Embellished Appliqué

for artful accessories

Patricia Converse

Creative Publishing international

Chanhassen, MN

Creative Publishing international

Copyright 2007
Creative Publishing international
18705 Lake Drive East
Chanhassen, Minnesota 55317
1-800-328-3895
www.creativepub.com
All rights reserved

President/CEO: Ken Fund
VP Sales & Marketing: Peter Ackroyd
Publisher: Winnie Prentiss
Executive Managing Editor: Barbara Harold
Development Editor: Sharon Boerbon Hanson
Photo Stylist: Joanne Wawra
Creative Director: Michele Lanci-Altomare
Art Director: Brad Springer
Photographers: Steve Galvin, Rudy Calin, Andrea Rugg
Production Manager: Laura Hokkanen
Illustrator: Deborah Pierce
Page Design and Layout: Brian Donahue/ bedesign, inc.

Library of Congress Cataloging-in-Publication
Converse, Patricia.
  Embellished appliqué for artful accessories : 20
machine-stitched projects for fashion items and personal
gifts / Patricia Converse.
     p. cm.
ISBN-13: 978-1-58923-296-9 (soft cover)
ISBN-10: 1-58923-296-8 (soft cover)
 1. Appliqué--Patterns. 2. Fancy work. I. Title.
  TT779.C63 2007
  746.44'5041--dc22   2006032898

Printed in China
10 9 8 7 6 5 4 3 2 1

Contents

A Time to Explore

Welcome to *Embellished Appliqué for Artful Accessories*. The twenty projects in this book bring embellished appliqué into your daily life through personal accessories. Beauty and adornment enrich our lives. In these pages, you will discover a range of techniques for machine appliqué that turn functional items into a wealth of artful delights. With the addition of creative and contemporary appliqué, practical items become feminine and elegant accessories, bringing more enjoyment to your life.

All the projects take appliqué beyond expectation. Each contains a *Designer's Secret*, special professional tricks and tips that work well. The tips can be applied to more than one project. Very detailed information on how the specific look of each project was achieved is included, so *Embellished Appliqué for Artful Accessories* works as a resource for exploring your own ideas. The complete patterns, instructions, techniques, and supply suggestions offer all you need for the successful completion of each beautiful accessory. In fact, most projects include how to make the accessory as well as the embellishment!

You will be able to easily adapt the techniques and patterns to your own designs, using a variety of fabrics, beads, crystals, and threads. The skills acquired from the completion of the projects will give you confidence in exploring embellished appliqué further.

My personal goal is to inspire you to explore machine appliqué. For me, the thread and the embellishments make a piece "sing." I find what works through experimentation, and I encourage you always to be open to something different, whether fabric, thread, stitch, or embellishment. Go outside your comfort zone—experiments on scraps may become the best thing you have ever done. Be open to serendipity.

I hope you will enjoy creating the designs in this book as much as I have enjoyed creating them for you. I am very grateful to Jane A. Sassaman, an inspirational teacher, and I recommend her book *The Quilted Garden* to anyone looking for further study.

Patricia Converse

Supplies, Tools, and Embellishments

Always give yourself the best tools and materials possible. Good supplies make creating beautiful embellishments faster and easier. The instructions for all projects in *Embellished Appliqué for Artful Accessories* assume you have basic sewing supplies when you begin a project, including a fabric marker, cutting mat, ruler, rotary cutter, iron, 9" × 12" (22.9 × 30.5 cm) tracing paper, and a chalk pencil.

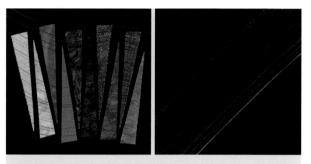

Threads

The possibilities in threads expand daily with cotton, polyester, rayon, monofilament, and silk in various weights. Weight refers to thickness, which means heavy threads may require a larger sewing machine needle. Threads take on a different aspect when stitched against fabrics. Experiment with different colors and stitches to discover possibilities. Always purchase good quality threads for machine sewing, and beading thread, which is stronger than regular thread, for handstitching beads.

Fusible Web

Fusible web permanently glues one fabric to another. Use it to hold small pieces of appliqué in place while stitching to avoid distortion. It usually comes with the web attached to one sheet of removable paper; occasionally it is sandwiched between two sheets of paper. To use it, trace the pattern onto the backing paper (remove the second paper if any), place the web on the wrong side of the appliqué fabric, and iron to fuse. Cut out the appliqué, remove the remaining paper, place the web on the ground fabric, and iron to fuse. Fusible web comes in different weights offering varied degrees of stiffness. Always test fusible web on a scrap of project fabric before beginning, and follow the manufacturer's instructions.

Fabric Glue

Use small amounts of fabric glue to hold a folded or raw edge in place for stitching. Gluing is faster than hand-basting and preserves the hand of soft fabrics. Choose acid-free stick glue that washes out. For a temporary bond, use basting glue. Test all glues on a scrap of project fabric for bleed-through, feel, and ease of use.

Fabrics

Today we have, literally, a world of fabric to choose from, each providing special characteristics. Cottons offer stability, are easy to sew, and come in a variety of prints and colors. Special-occasion fabrics offer variety in hand and texture but require careful attention to the manufacturer's recommended iron temperature and washing instructions. Knit fabrics require special handling. Most projects in *Embellished Appliqué for Artful Accessories* use woven cotton. Choose a fabric suitable to the project, and remember to check out bargain sections for rare finds.

Aerosol Spray Baste

Use spray baste to hold pieces of fabric, stabilizers, or patterns in place for stitching. The fabrics retain their hand even though the spray is permanent. Always test spray baste on a scrap of project fabric to ensure that unwanted residue doesn't remain when the paper or stabilizer is removed.

Removable Stabilizers

A removable stabilizer provides a smooth backing to fabric, allowing for precise stitching. Place one between the machine throat plate and the fabric, or on the wrong side of the fabric. When all the stitching is completed, remove the stabilizer. Removable stabilizers, in various weights, come in tear-away, water-soluble, and self-adhesive forms. Experiment to find what works for your project and fabric.

Interfacing

Use fusible interfacing (light, medium, or heavy weight) as a permanent stabilizer for stitching and fabrics. To choose the proper weight for suitable stiffness, test one layer with a piece of project fabric. Recommended weights are listed for each project. Follow the manufacturer's instructions and always test interfacings on scraps of project fabric. Double-sided stiff fusible interfacing is used for boxes, bags, and the belt, as it provides the proper stiffness. It is too stiff to stitch into a seam, so cut it to fit within the fabric stitching lines and fuse it to the wrong side of the fabric. Stitch the seam along its edge, through the fabric only. Use a larger needle for successful decorative machine stitching.

Sewing Machine

A standard domestic sewing machine and straight, zigzag, and buttonhole stitches were used for the projects. Choose the right needle for each fabric (usually a size 10 or 12 and occasionally a 16). The tension is very important when doing decorative stitching; test the tension on fabric scraps before stitching and adjust as required.

Open-Toe Machine Embroidery Foot

This sewing machine foot has no crosspiece in front of the needle and offers clear visibility for stitching. A groove in the foot just behind the needle allows heavily stitched areas to pass freely. This foot is especially helpful when stitching very small or tightly curved designs.

Even Feed or Walking Machine Foot

This sewing machine attachment or option allows all the layers being sewn to feed through the sewing machine at the same rate. This is very useful when quilting, in order to achieve a smoothly stitched piece.

Light Box

A light box has a translucent top and internal light source. It is used when tracing patterns. Turn the light on. Tape the pattern to the light box with removable tape, and tape the fabric over the pattern. This works well with light or transparent fabrics. You may also use a window the same way.

Irons

A standard household steam iron was used for all of the projects. Watch iron temperatures when working with interfacings, fusible web, and special-occasion fabrics. Do not stretch the fabrics, simply press lightly. A mini iron has a surface about 1" (2.5 cm) long, which is helpful for small details.

Beads

Use beading thread, not sewing thread, as it is more resistant to abrasion and less likely to break. Choose a neutral color in a weight that passes easily through the smallest bead hole (especially when passing through twice) and supports the weight of the beads. Beading needles are essential for working with beads that have very small holes, such as seed beads. Most of the beads and beading supplies used in *Embellished Appliqué for Artful Accessories* were purchased from Fire Mountain Gems and Beads, www.firemountaingems.com, and the others were purchased at craft and sewing stores.

Crystals

Cut-glass crystals come in a variety of colors, finishes, and sizes, which are given in millimeters (mm). Hot-fix crystals (rhinestones) come pre-glued. A heating tool is required to melt the glue backing. Crystals can be glued in place with glue made for crystals. Be sure to follow the manufacturer's instructions. The crystals used in *Embellished Appliqué for Artful Accessories* were purchased from Creative Crystal Co., www.creative-crystal.com.

Techniques

Machine appliqué adds surface design to a ground fabric. This section explains the techniques used in *Embellished Appliqué for Artful Accessories*. Hints on using the techniques in other ways are included with many projects.

Pattern Placement Using Tracing Paper

Use tracing paper if the ground fabric is dark. Trace all pattern lines onto tracing paper. Place the traced pattern on the ground fabric and hold in place with weights. Slip the sections of previously cut and prepared elements between the layers and adjust until they align with the drawing. Remove the tracing paper. Glue, fuse, or pin the elements in place for stitching.

Pattern Placement Using a Motif Cutout

Use a motif cutout when placement flexibility is desired. Trace only the outside edge of the design

Stitching

Stitching is as important to appliqué as a pencil stroke is to drawing. It defines shapes, connects elements, and provides texture, color, and interest. The stitching also holds fabrics together and finishes fabric edges. Fine machine appliqué stitching is both functional and aesthetic.

Precise, tidy stitching gives work a finished look. Use scraps of the ground and appliqué fabrics to rehearse threads, stitching length and width, color, and texture. Always pull all threads to the back, knot, and trim. Save money by using decorative thread in the needle and a similar color standard thread in the bobbin. Use a stabilizer for precise stitching.

All of the projects in this book have finished edges, most often sewn with a zigzag stitch. Experiment before beginning the project to achieve the look desired.

onto paper and cut it out. Place the cutout on the ground fabric. Draw a chalk or removable pencil line around the cutout. Assemble the previously cut and prepared design elements within the outline. Glue, fuse, or pin the elements in place for stitching.

Stitch Types
From top to bottom: Tight (often referred to as satin stitch). Loose. Wide. Narrow.

Varied-Width Zigzag Stitch
Adjust the stitch width every few stitches to create a narrow to wide effect.

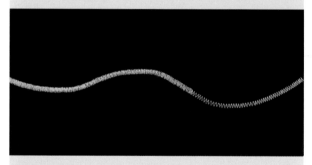

Zigzag Rope
Stitch a zigzag line, then overstitch with a slightly wider zigzag stitch.

Monofilament on Thread
Stitch a zigzag line, then overstitch with monofilament.

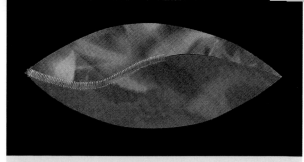

Intersection Overstitch
Satin stitch over the intersection of two fabrics.

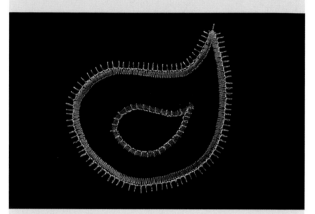

Combo Stitch
Stitch a zigzag line, then stitch alongside or over it with a buttonhole stitch.

Creating Depth
Stitch all "underneath" or "in back" design elements first. Next stitch the "on top" elements and stitch over the ends of the underneath stitching to create the illusion of depth.

Organic Form Stitching
Straight stitch a main stem, then add each small branch in a gentle arc (avoid right angles). Satin stitch the small branches using a thinner zigzag than the main stem, if applicable to the design.

Stitching Shapes

When stitching a very tight zigzag to make a satin stitch, a looser tension on the top thread often helps avoid puckering. Keep stitching smooth and consistent; the needle should fall just outside of the top fabric.

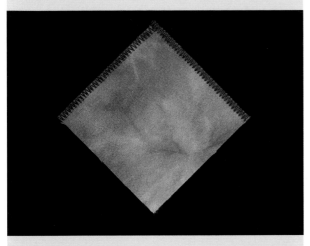

Outside Corners

Stitch to the corner, ending with the needle down on the outside. Turn the work and continue stitching.

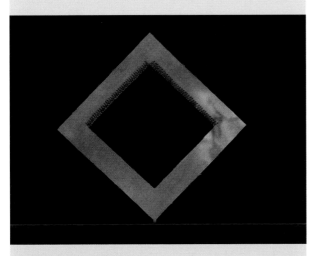

Inside Corners

Stitch to the corner, ending with needle down on the inside. Turn the work and continue stitching.

Points

Most of the projects in this book taper the width of the zigzag to fit a point on the appliqué motif by reducing the stitch width every few stitches.

Circles

To zigzag stitch a tight, smooth, round circle, stitch very slowly and pivot frequently. Always stop with the needle down on the outside of the circle and raise the presser foot to pivot.

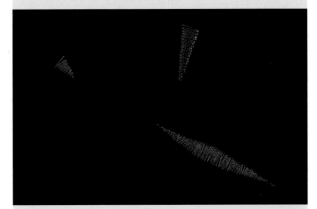

Triangles

Form a triangle by widening or narrowing the stitch width every two or three stitches.

Altering

Use a straight stitch to subtly change the color or texture of fabric.

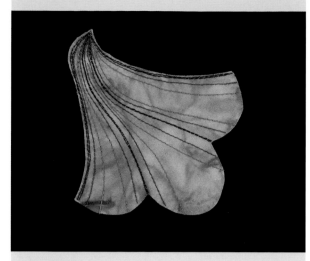

Detailing
Use a straight stitch to provide details that define your design.

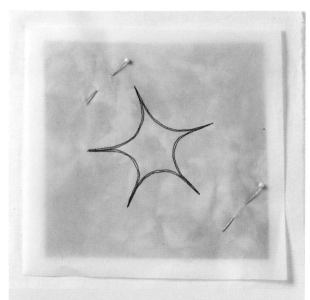

Stitch and Cut-Away, Step 1
Three fabrics are used for this technique: a ground, a reveal, and a design fabric. Rough cut all fabrics larger than required. Lay the ground fabric right side up, place the reveal fabric right side up in the desired location, and lay the design fabric right side up over it. Trace the cut-away motif onto tracing paper. Place the traced design over the design fabric. Pin all layers together. Straight stitch, just a hair outside the design lines, through all layers. Remove the tracing paper.

Random Stitching
Create random stitching by lowering the feed dogs on the sewing machine and moving the fabric. Random stitching adds color or texture and interest to a design.

Stitch and Cut-Away, Step 2
Trim away the design fabric as close to the stitching as possible with a small, sharp scissors. Overstitch the design edge with a zigzag or other decorative stitch. Press.

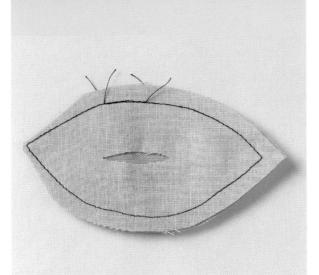

Stitch and Turn, Step 1

Appliqué takes on dimension with this technique. Fold the fabric right sides together. Pin a traced pattern to the fabric and cut it out. Stitch the two pieces together, right sides facing. Cut a small turning slit in the back piece.

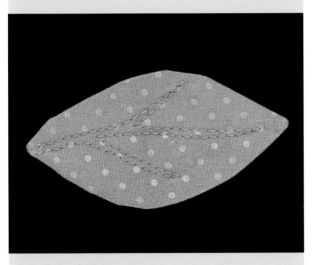

Stitch and Turn, Step 2

Turn the shape through the slit; press. Use a blind stitch to apply the motif to the design.

Templates

A template is a guide in the shape of a design or piece of a motif. Often templates are placed on the wrong side of the fabric, so they are created as a reverse of the design piece.

Fusible Interfacing, Step 1

Use this technique to make appliqué pieces with a folded edge. The interfacing adds stiffness, so use this technique when this is desired. Place the appliqué pattern under the interfacing. Trace the appliqué pattern (without seam allowance) on the right side of the interfacing.

Fusible Interfacing, Step 2

Place the interfacing on the wrong side of the chosen fabric, glue side down. Adhere to the fabric following the manufacturer's instructions. Add a ¼" (6 mm) seam allowance and cut out the pattern. Fold the fabric smoothly over the interfacing. Clip the fabric close to the fold line on inside points and across the seam allowance to ease the fabric around curves. Hold the folded edge in place with fabric-safe glue, hand basting, or careful pressing.

Fusible Interfacing, Step 3
Place the motif in the design and stitch in place with a straight or decorative stitch as the project dictates.

Fusible Web, Step 3
Fuse the design fabric to the ground fabric following the manufacturer's instructions. Topstitch and overstitch.

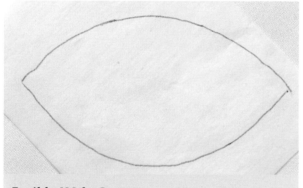

Fusible Web, Step 1
Use fusible web for small pieces. Fusible web is used exclusively in *Embellished Appliqué for Artful Accessories* for pieces with raw edges finished by surface stitching, usually zigzag. Refer to *Fusible Web* (page 00). Fusible web comes with one or two sheets of removable paper. Trace the pattern onto the covering paper.

Fusible Web, Step 2
Remove the paper on the glue side, if necessary, and place the pattern on the wrong side of the design fabric. Fuse following the manufacturer's instructions. Cut the paper, web, and fabric along the pattern lines.

Freezer Paper, Step 1
Use this technique to make appliqué pieces with a folded edge. The freezer paper provides a shape to fold the seam allowance against and will be removed before stitching. Use this technique when no stiffness is desired in the applied fabric. Place the freezer paper shiny side down over the appliqué pattern. Trace the outside edge of the pattern without seam allowance. A light box may be helpful for tracing.

Freezer Paper, Step 2

Place the freezer paper, shiny side down, on the wrong side of the design fabric and adhere with a warm dry iron. Add a ¼" (6 mm) seam allowance and cut out the pattern. Fold the fabric smoothly over the paper. Clip the fabric close to the fold line on inside points, and across the seam allowance to ease the fabric around curves. Hold the folded edge in place by lightly using spray starch on the wrong side and pressing.

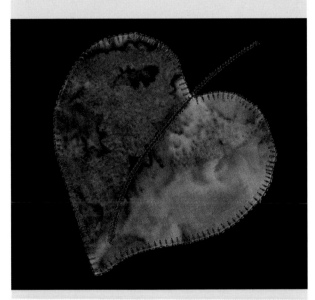

Freezer Paper, Step 3

Remove the freezer paper. Place the appliqué on the larger work and stitch in place with straight or decorative stitching.

Beading

Beading adds texture and color to appliqué. Refer to *Beads* (page 6).

Basic Attachment

Begin and end beading by taking a few small stitches on the wrong side of the project with a beading needle and beading thread. To hand-stitch a single bead, use a running stitch. Bring the needle and thread up to the right side, through the bead, and down to the wrong side.

Fringe and Freehanging

Create fringe or attach freehanging beads by bringing the needle and thread to the right side of the fabric, then through all the beads. Skip the end bead, which acts as the anchor, and return the thread through all the remaining beads and the fabric.

Beading a Fringe

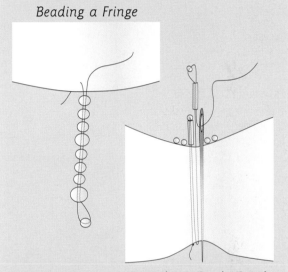

Attaching Bugle Beads

Backstitched Attachment

Firmly secure individual beads with backstitching. Place the end bead in position on the front face of the fabric. Bring the needle and thread up to the right side of the fabric to the left of the bead. Pick up the bead on the needle, and then insert the needle back through the fabric on the right side of the bead. Bring the needle up to the front face of the fabric two bead widths along, and pick up the second bead. Repeat the return, and continue the procedure until all beads are placed. This technique works well when precise bead placement is required.

Backstitching

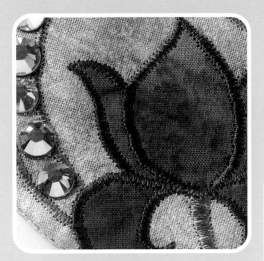

Amulet Bag

Amulet bags are considered jewelry. This charming piece features a crystal bead necklace holding a diminutive bag enhanced with satin stitching and sparkly crystals. Pearls, gemstones, or healing stones offer other looks and one-of-a-kind personalization. The number of beads and crystals needed will depend on the length of the necklace. To ensure the elegance of your design, always pull all threads to the back, knot, and trim.

The flower pattern is reversed because you will fuse it to fusible web, then to the wrong side of the fabric. When cut out, it will appear in the right orientation.

Refer to *Fabrics* and to *Threads* (page 5); to *Removable Stabilizers*, to *Light Box*, and to *Crystals* (page 6); *Stitching* (page 7); *Stitching Shapes* (page 9); *Fusible Web* (page 12); and *Beading* (page 13) before beginning. Test thread colors, stitch lengths, and stitch widths on fabric scraps.

When using any fusible product, always follow the manufacturer's instructions.

Materials

- Bag/lining fabric, 12" (30.5 cm) square
- Paper-backed fusible web, 4" (10.2 cm) square
- Flower fabric, 4" (10.2 cm) square
- Light box
- Removable stabilizer, 4" (10.2 cm) square
- Threads

- Thirty-two Aurora Borealis crystals, nine 7 mm, five 6 mm, and eighteen 4 mm
- Round beads, gray 4 mm, silver 4 mm
- Crystal beads, purple 6 mm, clear 4 mm
- Beading thread
- Beading needle

1 Trace and transfer the bag pattern (page 17) using your favorite method. Cut four bag/lining fabric circles.

2 Trace the outline of the flower pattern (page 17) onto tracing paper and cut it out. Draw around the pattern on the fusible web paper-backing. Adhere the web to the wrong side of the flower fabric, leaving the backing intact. Cut the pattern out along the traced lines.

3 Trace the leaves and flower patterns (page 17) onto the right side of one circle, using a light box and a lead or colored pencil. Stitching will cover the lines.

4 Place the removable stabilizer under this circle, then zigzag stitch the edges of the leaves.

5 Remove the paper-backing and fuse the flower to the fabric circle. Zigzag stitch around the flower. Create the stem with a varied-width zigzag stitch. Remove the stabilizer.

6 Pin the completed circle to another circle, right sides together. Stitch the circles together with a ¼" (6 mm) seam, leaving an opening for turning. Repeat with the remaining circles. Trim all seams to ⅛" (3 mm). Turn, then press the circles.

7 Add the crystals using the illustration (page 17) as a guide and following the manufacturer's instructions.

8 Blindstitch the openings in both circles closed; then blindstitch the circles together, leaving an opening, to create the bag.

9 On the beading needle, secure a length of beading thread long enough for the necklace. Pull the needle through from the inside of the bag. Add beads as desired. To follow the main beading pattern in the example shown, pick up 3 silver, 1 gray, 1 clear, 1 gray, 2 clear, *1 purple, 2 clear, 1 gray, 1 clear, 1 gray, 3 silver, 1 clear, 3 silver, 1 gray, 1 clear, 1 gray, 2 crystal, 1 purple. Repeat from * as needed to complete the necklace, ending with the reverse of the sequence before the *. Pull the needle to the inside of the bag and secure the thread.

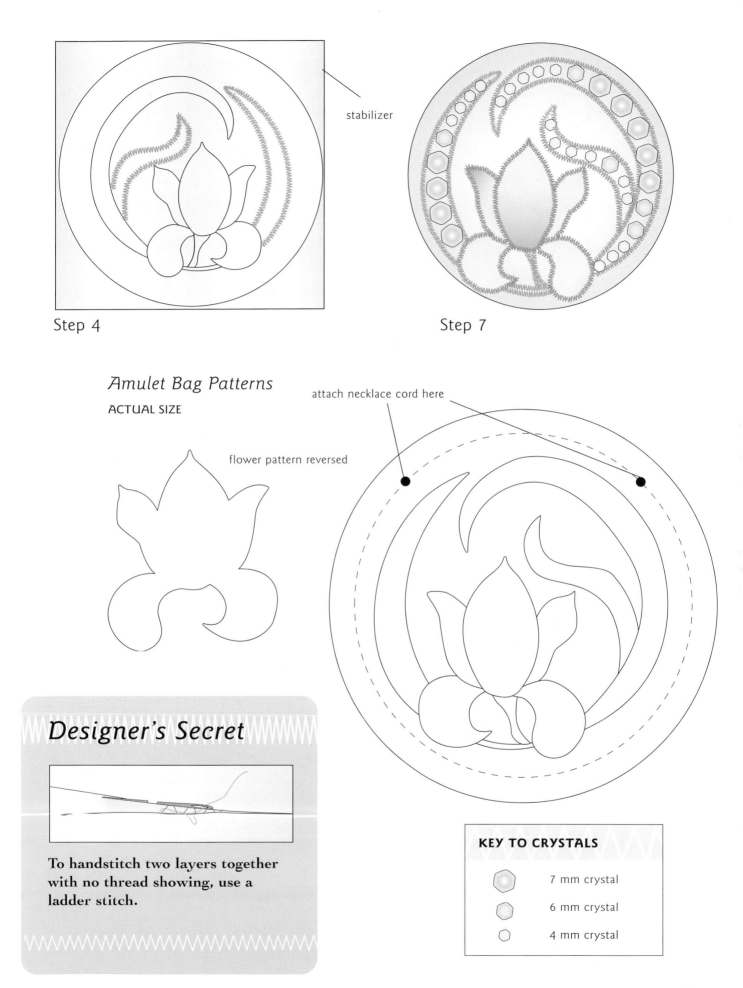

stabilizer

Step 4

Step 7

Amulet Bag Patterns
ACTUAL SIZE

flower pattern reversed

attach necklace cord here

Designer's Secret

To handstitch two layers together with no thread showing, use a ladder stitch.

KEY TO CRYSTALS

	7 mm crystal
	6 mm crystal
	4 mm crystal

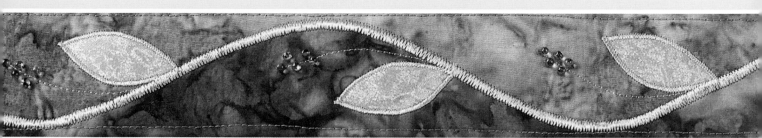

Two-Toned Belt

Fabric on fabric creates a stunning stained-glass effect. Understated stitchery and the glimmer of beads combine to encircle the wearer with art. The belt is constructed with double-sided stiff fusible interfacing for stability and a hook-and-loop tape closure.

Refer to *Fabrics* and to *Threads* (page 5); to *Removable Stabilizers* and to *Interfacing* (page 6); to *Stitching* (page 7); to *Fusible Web* (page 12); to *Stitching Shapes* (page 9); and to *Beading* (page 13) before beginning. Test thread colors, stitch lengths, and stitch widths on fabric scraps.

When using any fusible product, always follow the manufacturer's instructions.

Materials

- Two design fabrics, 4" (10.2 cm) × length of belt

- Double-sided stiff fusible interfacing, 2" (5.1 cm) × length of belt* minus 1" (2.5 cm)

- Paper-backed fusible web, 8" (20.3 cm) square

- Leaf fabric, 8" (20.3 cm) square

- Threads

- Two removable stabilizers, 2" (5.1 cm) square

- Fringe beads, gold and red 4 mm

- Beading thread

- Beading needle

- Lining fabric, 2" (5.1 cm) × length of belt*

- Two pieces ¾" (1.9 cm) long hook-and-loop tape, ⅝" (1.6 cm) wide

- Permanent adhesive, Fabri-Tac™

- Snaps or hooks (optional)

Note: To determine the length of a belt, measure the waist snugly and add 3" (7.6 cm).

1 Trace the belt pattern (page 21) onto tracing paper, repeating as needed to fill the entire belt length. Lay the design fabrics right sides up and all edges squared, one on top of the other. Place the pattern down the center and tape or pin in place on the edges. Cut along the center stem line. Discard the extra fabric or save it to make a second belt.

2 Fit both fabrics together on the interfacing, with ½" (1.3 cm) of seam allowance on both ends. Adhere the interfacing. Chalk or transfer the leaf and stem placement patterns as needed.

3 Trace the outline of the leaf pattern (page 21) onto tracing paper and cut it out. Draw around the pattern on the fusible web paper-backing, drawing as many leaves as needed. Adhere the web to the wrong side of the leaf fabric, leaving the backing intact. Cut the patterns out along the traced lines. Fuse them to the belt.

4 Stitch around all the leaves using a narrow zigzag stitch. Stitch the flower stems with straight stitches. Stitch the center stem with a wider zigzag stitch. Pull all threads to the back, knot, and trim. **Note:** The stitching for the center stem extends into the seam allowance. Put a small piece of removable stabilizer under both ends to keep the stitching stable. Remove them after stitching.

5 Handstitch the beads in place.

6 Trim the lining to the length of the interfacing. Adhere the lining to the interfacing.

7 Fold under the seam allowance ¼" (6 mm) and fold under again to the backside. Pin in place. Repeat on all sides, neatly folding the corners in. Topstitch ⅛" (3 mm) from all edges.

8 Adhere the loop-tape, with permanent adhesive, to the front side of one end and the hook-tape to the back side of the opposite end. Use snaps or hooks if you prefer.

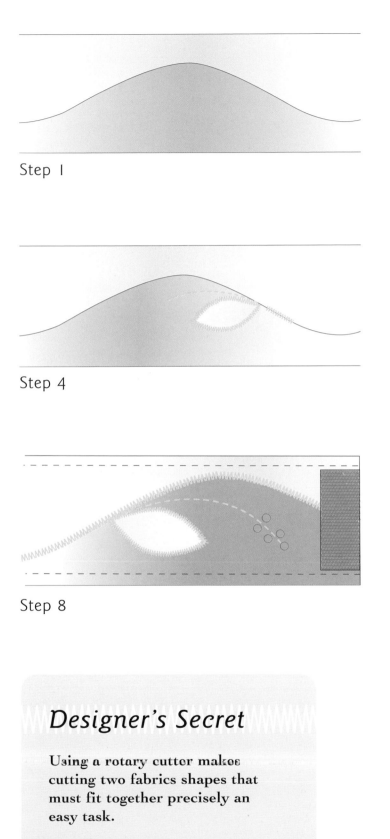

Step 1

Step 4

Step 8

Designer's Secret

Using a rotary cutter makes cutting two fabrics shapes that must fit together precisely an easy task.

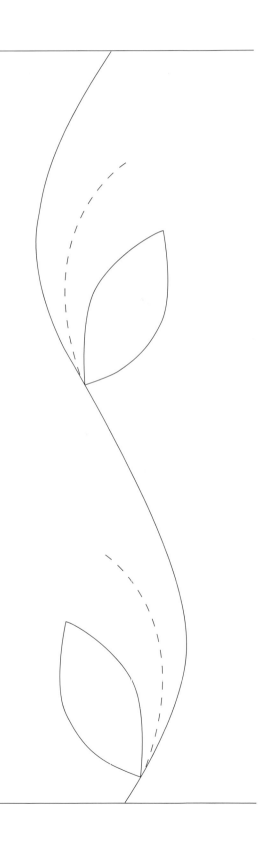

Blue-Green Scarf

J azz up a simple sweater or suit with this soft fashion scarf. The stylized flower and jewels add a focal point and designer-detailing interest.

Refer to *Fabrics* and to *Threads* (page 5); to *Aerosol Spray Baste*, to *Removable Stabilizers* and to *Crystals* (page 6); to *Stitching* (page 7); and to *Stitching Shapes* (page 9) before beginning. Rehearse thread colors, stitch lengths, and stitch widths on fabric scraps.

Materials

- Georgette or chiffon for scarf, 2 yd. (1.8 m)

- Aerosol spray baste

- Water-soluble stabilizer, 6" × 10" (15.2 × 25.4 cm)

- Photocopier

- Threads

- Flower fabric, soft fashion, 7" (17.8 cm) square

- Fifteen Aurora Borealis hot fix crystals, hyacinth 4 mm

Note: Georgette and chiffon come in easy-care polyester, with the soft hand perfect for a scarf. Cut the fabric lengthwise to achieve the proper drape. Two yards (1.8 m) of fabric make two or three scarves, depending on width.

1 Cut two scarf pieces, 72" × 8" (182.9 × 20.3 cm). Set one piece aside until step 13.

2 Apply spray baste to the stabilizer, covering an area 10" (25.4 cm) up from one end. Adhere the stabilizer to the wrong side of the fabric under the design area.

3 Trace the flower pattern (page 27), including the stem, the center vein of each flower petal, and the centerline guide. Make two copies on a photocopier.

4 Mark the vertical center of the scarf fabric with pins. Cut the excess paper away from the pattern for easier alignment of the pattern with the pins. Place the pattern on the right side of the fabric, aligning the centerline guide with the center of the fabric. Pin the pattern to the fabric.

5 Machine stitch both stems with a straight stitch in the appropriate thread color. Remove the paper pattern.

6 Place the second pattern on the right side of the flower fabric. Place a piece of scrap paper under the fabric, making a fabric sandwich. Pin all the layers together and cut out the flower.

7 Remove the scrap paper from the bottom. Spritz spray baste on the wrong side of the flower fabric. Place the flower pattern on the scarf fabric, using the stitched stem and the centerline guide to center it. Machine stitch the flower to the scarf, using a straight stitch in the appropriate thread color along the center veins. Remove the paper pattern.

8 Zigzag stitch the small stem using a narrow stitch. Zigzag stitch the large stem, extending the stem into the flower.

9 Use a chalk pencil to mark the individual flower petals and the additional lines on each petal. Stitch the additional lines following the center vein line, which echoes the outside petal line. This stitching mimics the way light falls on the petals and creates the illusion of dimension. Pull all threads to the back, knot, and trim.

Continued ⁝▸

tracing paper   scarf

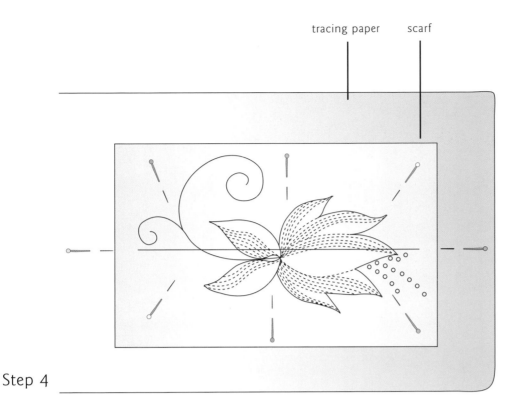

Step 4

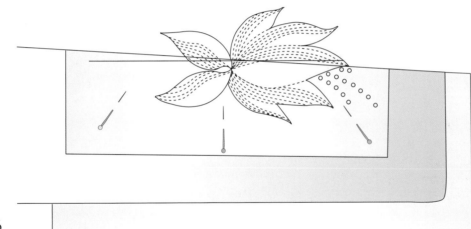

Step 6

Designer's Secret

Stabilize thin fabrics when cutting out small or intricate shapes by making a sandwich of scrap paper, fabric, and pattern pinned together.

Step 10

10 Zigzag stitch the petals in the order listed, using a varied-width stitch that is very small at the petal tips.

1: top right
2: top left, slightly overlapping the stem
3: bottom far right
4: bottom far left
5: center right
6: center left, stitching up to stem base
7: top center, from stem base to tip and back

11 Adhere the crystals in graceful arcs, as shown (page 27), following the manufacturer's instructions. **Note:** Put a piece of stabilizer under the wrong side of thin fabrics to catch any excess glue.

12 Pull off all stabilizer that can be removed; then follow the manufacturer's instructions to remove the remaining stabilizer with water. Allow the fabric to dry.

13 Place the scarf pieces right sides together and pin. Stitch the pieces together with a ½" (1.3 cm) seam. Leave an opening for turning. Trim the seams to ¼" (6 mm). Turn the scarf; then handstitch the opening closed. Lightly press.

centerline guide

KEY TO STITCHES & CUTTING

– – – – – – – – stitching
———————— cutting
WWWWWWWWWW zigzag stitch

Butterfly Evening Bag

The butterfly evening bag is a unique accessory for dressy social events. Made from sumptuous, special-occasion fabrics, it is the perfect complement to a prom dress, bridesmaid gown, or cocktail dress. This zippered pouch is just the right size—small enough to carry with ease but roomy enough for all the essentials. Shimmering beads and crystals give the butterfly its magical quality. A more casual butterfly bag could be made from cottons or linen and accented with wooden beads.

Refer to *Fabrics* and to *Threads* (page 5); to *Interfacing* and to *Crystals* (page 6); to *Stitching* (page 7); to *Fusible Web* (page 12); to *Stitching Shapes* (page 9); and to *Beading* (page 13) before beginning. Test thread colors, stitch lengths, and stitch widths on fabric scraps.

When using any fusible product, always follow the manufacturer's instructions.

Materials

- Medium-weight fusible interfacing, 1/3 yd. (0.3 m)
- Outer bag fabric, ⅓ yd. (0.3 m)
- Lining, ⅓ yd. (0.3 m)
- Paper-backed fusible web, 7" (17.8 cm) square
- Butterfly fabric, 8" (20.3 cm) square
- Threads
- Twenty crystals, clear, four 5 mm, sixteen 3 mm

- Iridescent seed beads, small package
- Six beads, silver, three 8 mm, three 4 mm
- Beading thread
- Beading needle
- Invisible zipper, 7" to 9" (17.8 to 22.9 cm)
- Cord for strap, ½ yd. (0.5 m)

1 Cut a piece of interfacing 22" × 11" (55.9 × 27.9 cm), and fuse it to the wrong side of the outer fabric, following the manufacturer's instructions. Trace the bag pattern (page 33) onto tracing paper and cut it out. Using the pattern, cut two bag pieces from both the outer fabric and the lining.

2 Trace the outline of the butterfly pattern (page 33) onto tracing paper and cut it out. Draw around the pattern on the fusible web paper-backing. Adhere the web to the wrong side of the butterfly fabric, leaving the backing intact. Cut the pattern out along the traced lines.

3 Fold one bag piece in half lengthwise, and mark the center line with pins. Remove the paper-backing from the butterfly. Fold the butterfly in half lengthwise and mark the center with pins. Center the butterfly on the bag piece, using the pins as a guide, and keeping the edges inside the seamlines indicated on the bag pattern. Fuse the butterfly to the bag front.

4 Stitch the design lines on the butterfly, using straight stitches and zigzag satin stitches as indicated in the illustration (page 31).

5 Adhere the crystals where indicated in the illustration, following the manufacturer's instructions.

6 Handstitch the beads to the wings, body, and antennae as indicated in the illustration.

7 Stitch one side of the invisible zipper to the upper edge of the bag front, aligning the tab to the side seamline and stitching on the ⅝" (1.6 cm) seamline of the upper edge. The zipper will be longer than the bag edge. Stop stitching at the opposite side seamline.

8 Stitch the opposite side of the zipper to the bag back. Close the zipper. With the right side of the bag facing up, front and back spread apart, bar tack across the zipper teeth even with the side seamline. Trim off the excess zipper ½" (1.3 cm) beyond the bar tack.

Continued ❖

Butterfly Evening Bag

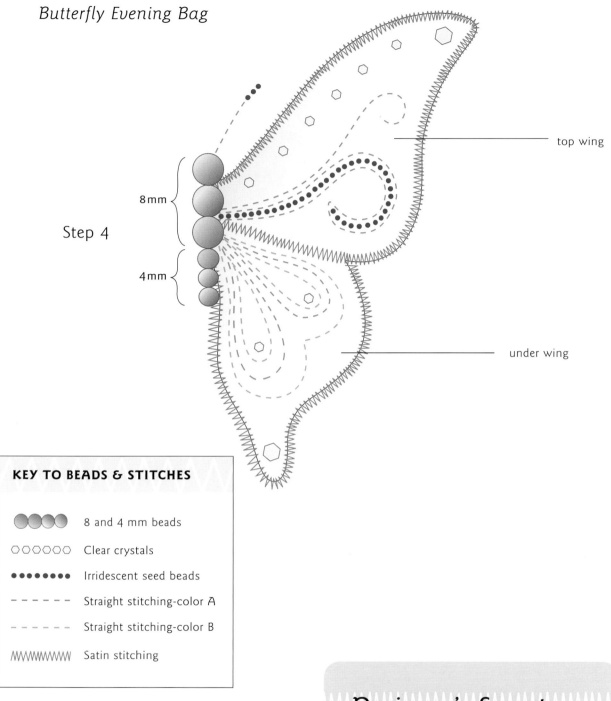

Step 4

8mm

4mm

top wing

under wing

KEY TO BEADS & STITCHES

⬤⬤⬤⬤ 8 and 4 mm beads

○○○○○ Clear crystals

●●●●●●● Irridescent seed beads

- - - - - Straight stitching-color A

- - - - - Straight stitching-color B

WWWWWWWW Satin stitching

Designer's Secret

To create the illusion of layered fabrics in a one-piece appliqué, stitch all the "back" items first. Overlap the previous stitching lines when you stitch the "front" items.

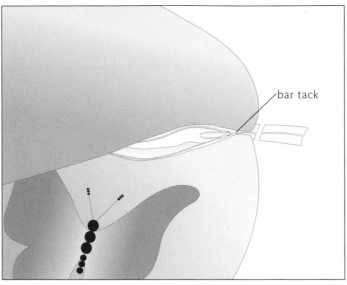

bar tack

Step 8

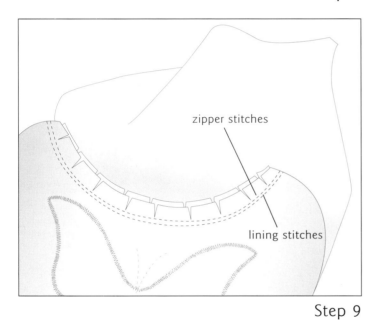

zipper stitches

lining stitches

Step 9

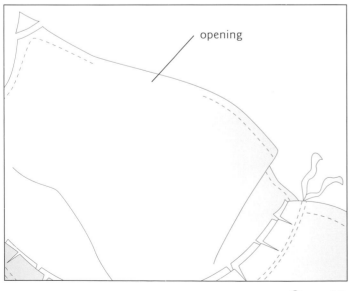

opening

Step 12

9 Pin a lining piece to the bag front along the upper edge, right sides together. With the bag front facing up, stitch ⅛" (3 mm) inside the zipper stitching line. Test the zipper to make sure the stitching is not too close to the zipper. Clip into the seam allowances up to, but not through, the stitching line.

10 Cut cording for the strap 1" (2.5 cm) longer than the desired length. Position the cord just below the zipper, with the ends extending over the side seam allowances. Baste the ends in place.

11 Pin the bag front and back right sides together. Stitch using a ¼" (6 mm) seam allowance. Clip into the seam allowances of the curves. Trim the seam allowances at the bottom point.

12 Open the zipper partway. Pin the lining pieces right sides together. Stitch the sides, leaving an opening for turning the bag. Clip into the seam allowances of the curves. Trim the seam allowances at the bottom point.

13 Turn the bag right side out through the opening. Stitch the opening closed.

Butterfly Evening Bag Patterns

ACTUAL SIZE

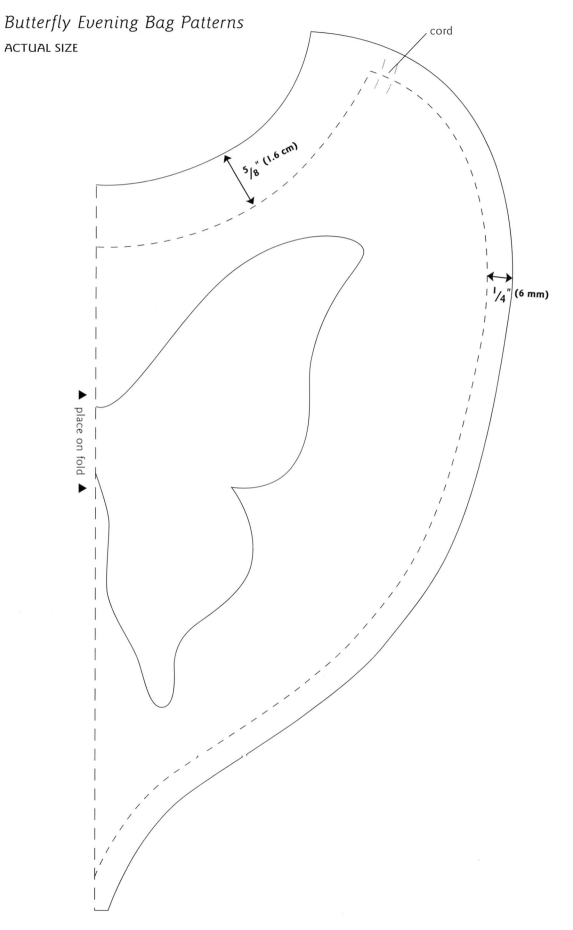

cord

5/8" (1.6 cm)

1/4" (6 mm)

◀ place on fold ▶

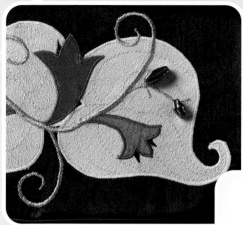

Pink Petals Clutch

Complement your little black dress perfectly with this elegant clutch. Special-occasion fabrics, gold metallic stitching on a black background, and the addition of bicone beads give just the right wow for an evening on the town.

The leaf and flower patterns are reversed. You will transfer them to fusible web, then fuse them to the wrong side of the fabrics. When cut out, they will appear in the right orientation.

Refer to *Fabrics* and to *Threads* (page 5); to *Interfacing* (page 6); to *Pattern Placement Using a Motif Cutout* and to *Stitching* (page 7); to *Stitching Shapes* (page 9); to *Fusible Web* (page 12); and to *Beading* (page 13) before beginning. Test thread colors, stitch lengths, and stitch widths on fabric scraps.

When using any fusible product, always follow the manufacturer's instructions.

Materials

Outer bag fabric, black, ¼ yd. (0.2 m)

Lining and small flowers fabric, pink, ¼ yd. (0.2 m)

Medium-weight fusible interfacing, ¼ yd. (0.2 m)

Paper-backed light-weight fusible web, 8" × 10" (20.3 × 25.4 cm)

Leaf fabric, 8" (20.3 cm) square

Threads

Four bicone beads, two 13 mm, two 8 mm

Beading needle

Beading thread

1 Cut a 15½" × 8" (39.4 × 20.3 cm) rectangle from the black and pink fabrics, and the fusible interfacing. Trace the bag's front curves pattern (page 41) onto tracing paper three times and cut each out. Pin a pattern on each of the rectangles, with the curves to the outside edges, and cut along the curves.

2 Trace the gusset pattern (page 39) onto tracing paper. Use the pattern to cut two pieces from each fabric and two pieces from the fusible interfacing.

3 Adhere the fusible interfacing to the wrong side of the black fabric and black gusset pieces.

4 Trace the outline of the flower and leaf patterns (pages 39 and 40) onto tracing paper and cut them out. Draw around the patterns on the fusible web paper-backing. Rough cut the patterns apart. Adhere the web to the wrong side of the appropriate flower and leaf fabrics, leaving the paper-backing intact. Cut the patterns out along the traced lines.

5 Trace the complete motif pattern (page 41) onto tracing paper and cut it out. Place the pattern on the right side of the bag fabric between the curved edges to use as a placement guide for the leaves. Draw around the motif with a chalk pencil. Fuse leaves A and B to the bag, using the chalked line as a guide. Zigzag stitch around both leaves, varying the width at the leaf tips.

6 Refer to the illustration and mark the leaf veins with a chalk pencil. Straight stitch the leaf veins.

7 Position the flowers over the leaves according to the pattern. Draw the connecting stems, trace the flower outlines, and indicate the background petals with the chalk pencil. Remove the flower pieces. Stitch a triangle to form each background petal.

8 Adhere the flowers over the leaves following the manufacturer's instructions; then zigzag stitch along all the edges.

Continued ⁖

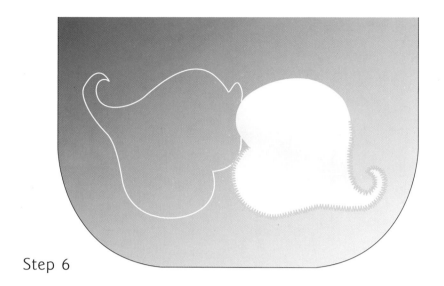

Step 6

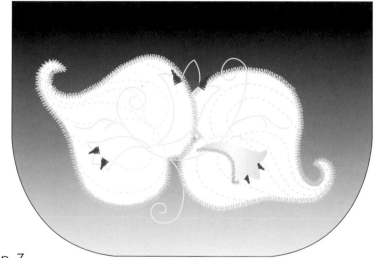

Step 7

Designer's Secret

Appliqué requires precise, even stitching for a finished look. A stabilizer or fusible interfacing gives the ground fabric the stability required for precise stitching.

9 Zigzag stitch a thin stem from the center stem outward, turn, and stitch back to the center stem over the same stitching. Repeat for each thin stem. Overstitch the main stem using a zigzag stitch and overstitch with a slightly wider zigzag (zigzag rope technique).

10 Handstitch the beads in place. Pull all threads to the back, knot, and trim.

11 Mark both sides of the bag along the edges at 5¼" (13.3 cm) in from the design end, then at 5⅛" (13 cm) and again at 4 ⅞" (12.4 cm).

12 Pin one black gusset to the bag, right sides together and matching mark A on the gusset to the second mark on the bag edge. Clip the curve within the seam allowance to allow the gusset to fit as needed. Stitch the gusset to the bag with a ¼" (6 mm) seam allowance. Repeat on the other side.

13 Repeat step 12 with the pink lining and gusset pieces.

14 Pin the lining to the bag, right sides together. Stitch the fabrics together, leaving an opening for turning. Clip the excess fabric at the inside corners at a 45 degree angle. Clip the outside curves as needed. Turn and press the bag. Handstitch the opening closed.

15 Pinch the gusset top edge together at the center. Stitch through all the layers to create a pleat in the gusset, which helps the bag hold its shape. Repeat on the other gusset.

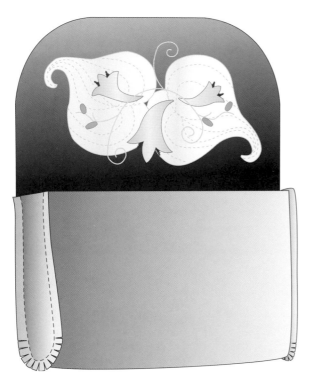

Step 12

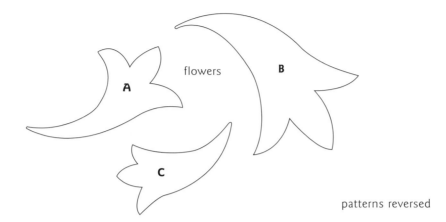

flowers

A

B

C

patterns reversed

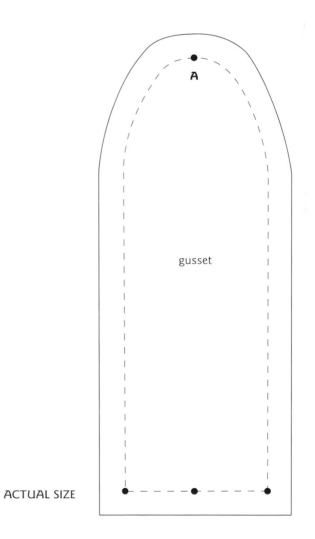

A

gusset

ACTUAL SIZE

Clutch Patterns
ACTUAL SIZE

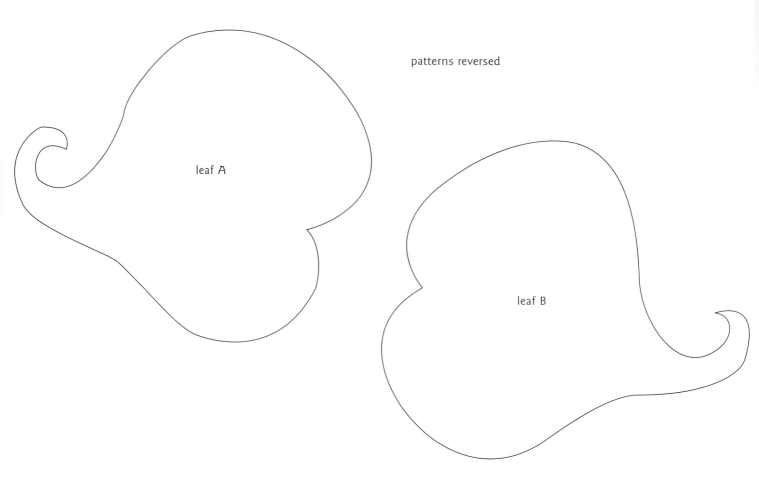

patterns reversed

leaf A

leaf B

Clutch Pattern

ACTUAL SIZE

◄ extend from here ◄

KEY TO STITCHES & CUTTING

————————	cutting
— — — — —	stitching
··················	outer edge/cutting

Flower Bud Pincushion

This pincushion is a bud ready to pop. It features fabric layered on fabric. The beaded center offers a glittery focal point. Use colors that coordinate with bedroom décor to create lovely gifts for friends and family.

Refer to *Fabrics* and to *Threads* (page 5); to *Stitching* (page 7); to *Stitching Shapes* (page 9); and to *Beading* (page 13) before beginning. Test thread colors, stitch lengths, and stitch widths on fabric scraps.

Materials

- Muslin ground fabric, 12" (30.5 cm) square
- Spray starch
- Quarter (coin)
- Inner bud and patterns A and B fabrics, three coordinating 4" (10.2 cm) squares
- Pattern C fabric, cotton 12" (30.5 cm) square
- Threads
- Twenty-one seed beads, eighteen gold, three red

- Beading needle
- Beading thread
- Fiberfill
- Three bugle beads, gold
- Extra-long hand-sewing needle, Dritz Quilting basting needle Gr7

Note: Cottons and special-occasion fabrics are good choices.

1 Lightly spray starch the muslin (for stability), then iron. Fold the fabric in quarters to find the center. Mark the center on both sides of the fabric.

2 Trace patterns A, B, and C, including the stitching lines and placement marks, onto tracing paper (page 47).

3 Place a quarter (coin) on the inner bud fabric. Draw around the coin with a pencil. Cut the fabric on the line. Place the circle, right side up, on the center of the ground fabric.

4 Lay pattern A on the right side of fabric A, and pin. Cut along the outer edge. Keeping the paper pattern in place, pin cutout A on the ground fabric over the small circle. Use the circle of placement marks for alignment. Straight stitch along the center pattern line through all the layers. Remove the tracing paper. Carefully cut fabric A out of the center, close to the stitched line. Zigzag stitch over the straight stitching, extending each point 1/8" (3 mm) to ¼" (6 mm).

5 Repeat step 4 with pattern and fabric B. Open the layers of fabric and carefully trim away excess fabric A.

6 Repeat step 4 with pattern and fabric C. Open the layers of fabric and carefully trim away excess fabric B and ground fabric.

7 Handstitch the seed beads to the inner bud fabric, leaving room in the very center to place the bugle beads (step 10).

8 With the right sides together, pin, and then stitch, the sections of C together. Turn right side out and stuff with fiberfill.

9 Trace the base pattern (page 46) onto tracing paper, pin to fabric C, and cut out. Fold under the edge of the base ¼" (6 mm) and hand-baste. Handstitch the base to the pincushion using a ladder stitch (refer to *Designer's Secret*, Amulet Bag, page 17). Remove the basting.

10 Handstitch the bugle beads to the center, using the extra-long needle. Pull the stitch from the base to the inner bud, picking up a bugle bead, then a red seed bead, then returning through the bugle bead to the base. Repeat for each bugle bead. This will compress the center slightly.

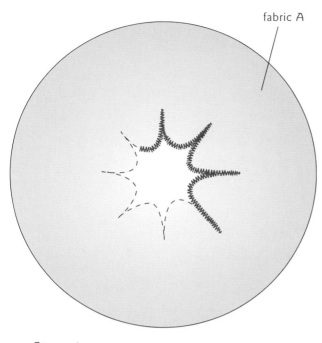

fabric A

Step 4

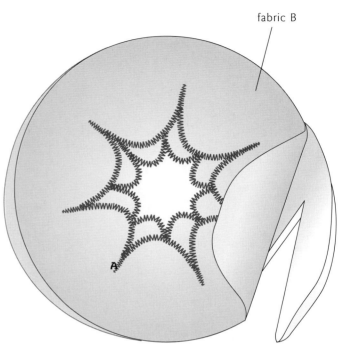

fabric B

Step 5

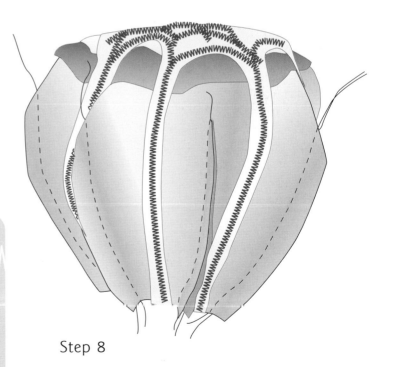

Step 8

Designer's Secret

A ground fabric can be used in place of stabilizer or interfacing to provide stability to decorative stitching.

Flower Bud Pincushion Pattern

ACTUAL SIZE

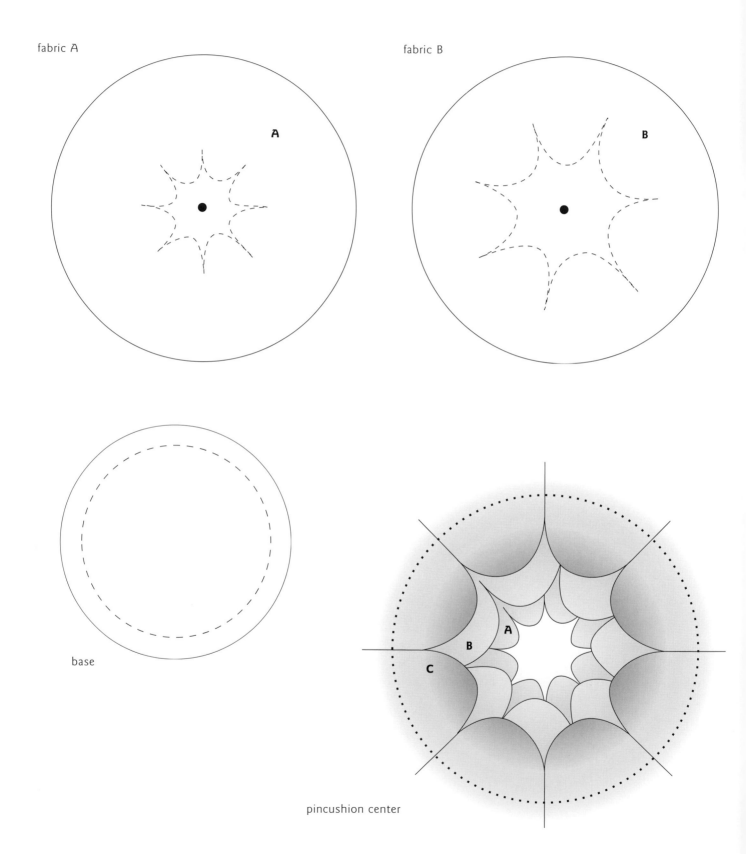

fabric A

A

fabric B

B

base

pincushion center

C

B

A

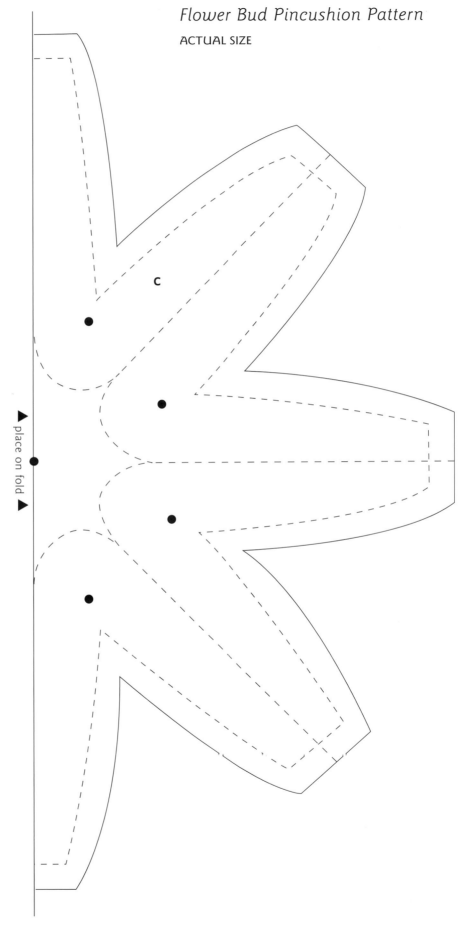

Flower Bud Pincushion Pattern
ACTUAL SIZE

C

▶ place on fold ▶

Foxglove Tee

Put some fun and creativity into your summer wardrobe. Turn a simple tee into a fashion statement with just one evening of stitching and beading.

The flower, leaf, and bud patterns are reversed. You will transfer them to fusible web, then fuse them to the wrong side of the fabrics. When cut out, they will appear in the right orientation.

Refer to *Fabrics* and to *Threads* (page 5); to *Aerosol Spray Baste*, to *Removable Stabilizers*, and to *Light Box* (page 6); *Pattern Placement Using Tracing Paper* and to *Stitching* (page 7); *Stitching Shapes* (page 9); *Fusible Web* (page 12); and to *Beading* (page 13) before beginning. Test thread colors, stitch lengths, and stitch widths on fabric scraps.

When using any fusible product, always follow the manufacturer's instructions.

Materials

- Bud fabric, 3" (7.6 cm) square
- Spray starch
- Threads
- Paper-backed fusible web, 8" (20.3 cm) square
- Light box
- Two flower fabrics, 4" (10.2 cm) square
- Aerosol spray baste

- Removable stabilizer, 4" × 9" (10.2 × 22.9 cm)
- Thirty-eight seed beads, thirty-three black, five gold
- Thirty-one pearl beads, 3 mm
- Beading thread
- Beading needle

Note: Use two tones of one color family for the flower fabrics.

1 Lightly spray starch the bud fabric. Stitch the fabric with a contrasting color thread in a grid pattern. Use short, straight stitches and sew the gridlines about ⅛" (3 mm) apart.

2 Trace the entire foxglove motif (page 51) onto tracing paper. Trace the outlines of the flower top, the base, and the bud patterns (page 51) onto the fusible web using a light box. Label them and roughly cut them out. Adhere the web to the wrong side of the appropriate fabrics, leaving the backing intact. Cut the patterns out along the traced lines.

3 Position, then pin, the tracing paper pattern onto the right side of the garment in the desired location. Spritz spray baste on one side of the removable stabilizer. Adhere the stabilizer to the wrong side of the garment in the pattern area, creating a sandwich of tracing paper, garment, and stabilizer. Be sure the stabilizer is under all the stitching areas.

4 Straight stitch the stems through all layers. Start under a flower, stitch to the end of the stem, turn, and stitch back over the stitching. Pull the threads to the back, knot, and trim.

5 Remove the paper-backing from the buds. Using the tracing paper as a guide, position the buds on the garment. Adhere to the garment and remove the tracing paper. Zigzag stitch around the edges.

6 Remove the paper-backing from the flower bases. Using the tracing paper as a guide, position the bases on the garment. Adhere to the garment and remove the tracing paper. Zigzag stitch the sides only.

7 Repeat step 5 with the flower tops. Remove the stabilizer.

8 Handstitch the black beads on one petal of each flower top. Create the small flowers with a gold-bead center surrounded by five pearls as shown in the photo. Create two additional small flowers, using three pearl beads for each.

Designer's Secrets

Fabric color and texture change subtly with overstitching. Stitch the fabric before or after cutting to create a different, yet coordinating fabric to use in a design.

When straight stitching tightly curved lines, a short stitch length makes smoother curves.

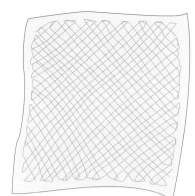

Step 1

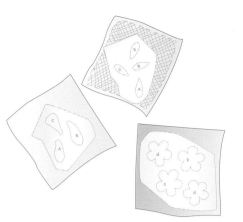

Step 2

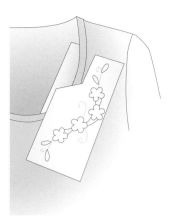

Step 3

Foxglove Tee Patterns

ACTUAL SIZE

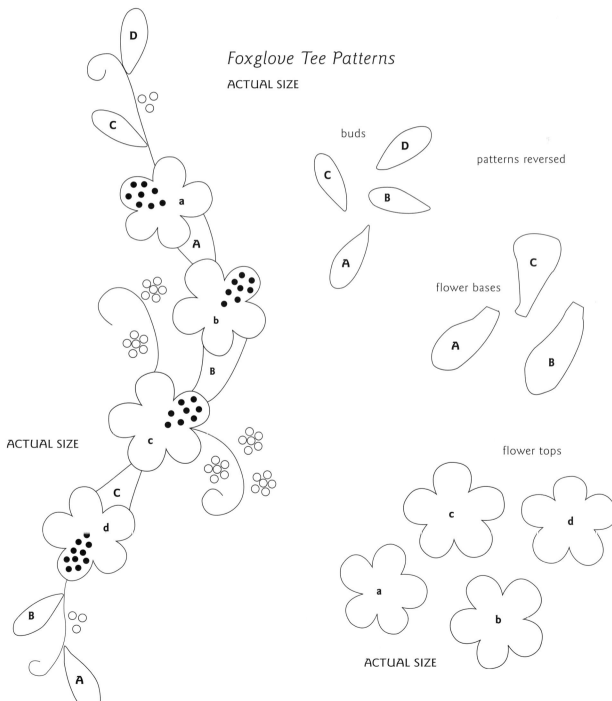

buds

patterns reversed

flower bases

flower tops

ACTUAL SIZE

ACTUAL SIZE

Hummingbird Box

Silver and blue iridescent threads and a jewel eye lend an air of fantasy to this triangular box with its glittery hummingbird. Double-sided stiff fusible interfacing opens up new possibilities for making shaped items.

Refer to *Fabrics* and to *Threads* (page 5); to *Aerosol Spray Baste*, to *Removable Stabilizers*, to *Interfacing*, and to *Crystals* (page 6); to *Stitching* (page 7); *Stitching Shapes* (page 9); and to *Fusible Web* (page 12) before beginning. Test thread colors, stitch lengths, and stitch widths on fabric scraps.

When using any fusible product, always follow the manufacturer's instructions.

Materials

- Tracing paper, 18" × 24" (45.7 × 61 cm)
- Outer box fabric, ½ yd. (0.5 m)
- Lining fabric, ½ yd. (0.5 m)
- Double-sided stiff fusible interfacing, 12" × 24" (30.5 × 61 cm)
- Paper-backed fusible web, 7" (17.8 cm) square

- Hummingbird fabric, 7" (17.8 cm) square
- Aerosol spray baste
- Removable stabilizer, 8" (20.3 cm) square
- Threads
- One crystal, pink, 4 mm

1 Enlarge the patterns (pages 56 and 57) by 125 percent. Draw a line vertically down the center of a sheet of tracing paper. Place the line along the midline of the box top pattern, and trace all lines. Turn the paper over and trace to develop the complete pattern. Enlarge the pattern 125 percent. Cut it out.

2 The outer pattern line indicates the outer fabric; the second line indicates the lining; and the inner line indicates the interfacing. Only one tracing is necessary if you cut the material in the order given. Position, then pin, the pattern on the outer fabric, and cut it out. Repeat on the lining fabric, then on the interfacing. Repeat steps 1 and 2 for the box base.

3 Trace the hummingbird (page 57) onto tracing paper and cut it out. Reverse the pattern, then draw around it on the fusible web paper-backing. Adhere the web to the wrong side of the hummingbird fabric, leaving the backing intact. On the right side of the hummingbird, mark the straight-stitching lines with chalk or removable marker. Cut the pattern out along the traced lines.

4 Carefully position the hummingbird on the right side of the box fabric, with the wings extended toward the top of the triangle. Fuse the hummingbird to the box fabric. Spritz spray baste on one side of the removable stabilizer. Adhere the stabilizer to the wrong side of the box fabric, under the hummingbird. Be sure the stabilizer is under all stitching areas.

5 Stitch the outside edges of the hummingbird's body with a narrow zigzag stitch, using a matching thread. Stitch the back wing and then the front wing, using a narrow zigzag stitch and silver thread. The front wing edges extend into the body. Straight stitch the wing details with silver thread. Highlight the upper body and head with random stitching in iridescent thread. Stitch the beak with silver thread, starting at the body with a wide zigzag and narrowing the stitching to a point. The beak may require overstitching to fill it in. Pull all threads to the back, knot, and trim. Remove the stabilizer.

6 Adhere the wrong side of the outer fabric to the double-sided fusible interfacing.

7 Center the lining on the wrong side of the outer fabric, over the interfacing, and fuse.

8 Fold one set of adjacent corner lines together, matching the interfacing edges, right sides of the outer fabric together, and pin. Stitch along the edge of the interfacing on the inside of the box. This will look like a dart. Repeat for all corners. *Continued* ⁘

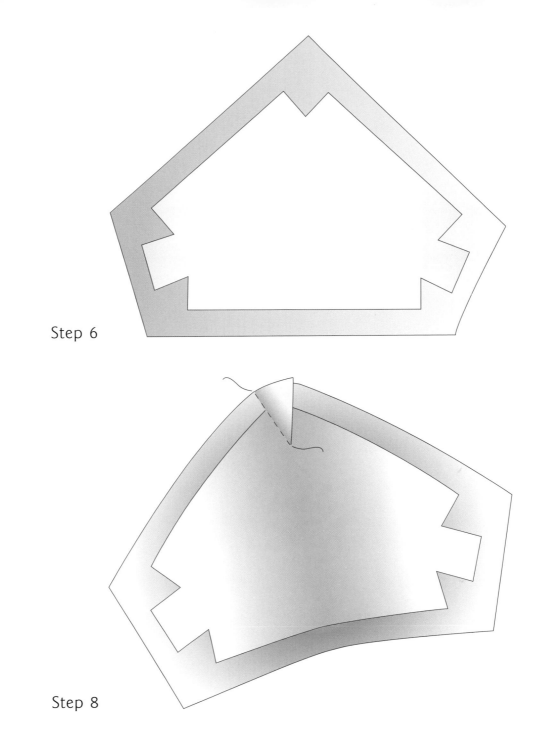

Step 6

Step 8

Designer's Secret

Threads create interest and
mood. Matching the thread color
to the fabric makes it disappear.
Metallic and iridescent threads
create a fantasy.

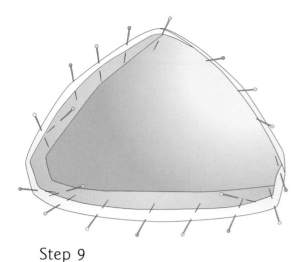

Step 9

9 Finish the edge of the box top by folding the outer fabric to the inside along the top of the interfacing. Fold again to cover the raw edge, and pin. Topstitch the folded edge in place. Press the box top to square the shape.

10 Repeat steps 6 to 9 to construct the box base.

11 Adhere the crystal, using the photo as a guide and following the manufacturer's instructions.

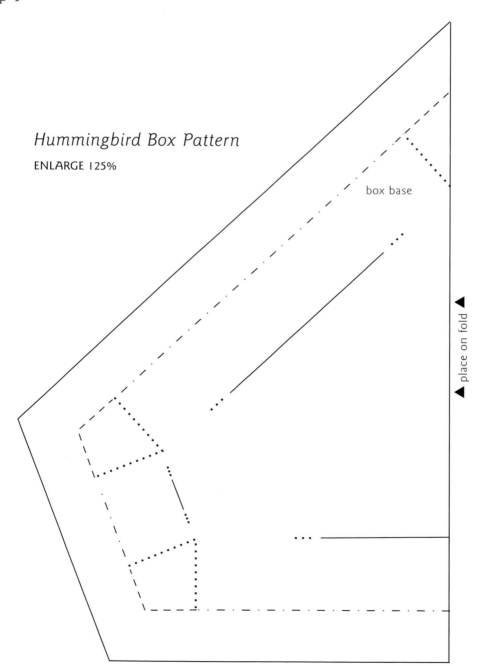

Hummingbird Box Pattern

ENLARGE 125%

box base

◄ place on fold ◄

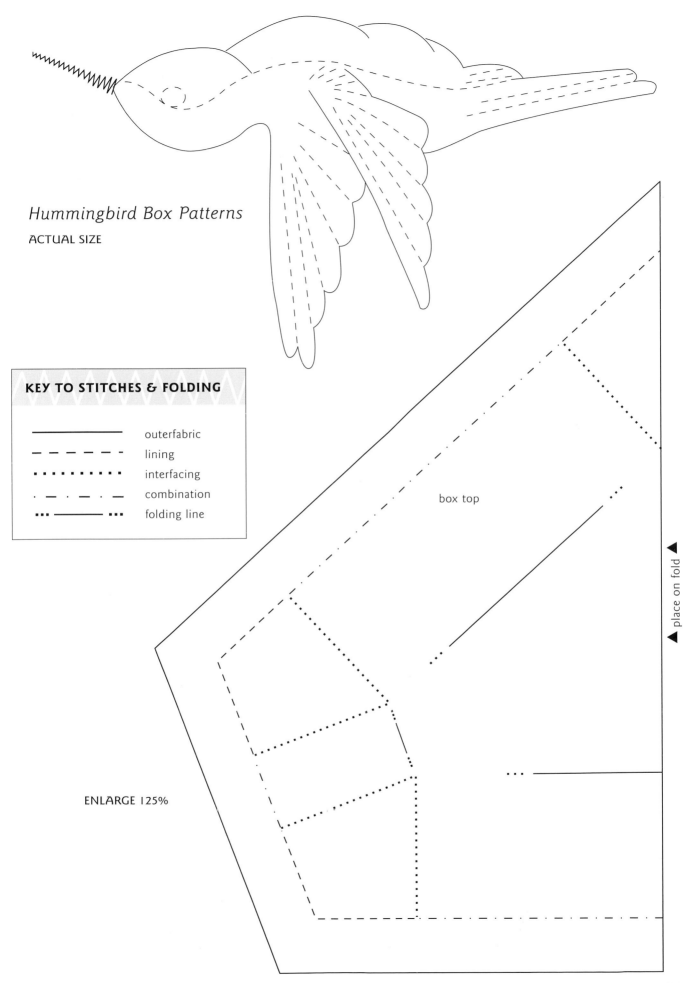

Hummingbird Box Patterns

ACTUAL SIZE

KEY TO STITCHES & FOLDING

——————	outerfabric
– – – – –	lining
•••••••••	interfacing
– · – · – ·	combination
••• —— •••	folding line

box top

◀ place on fold ◀

ENLARGE 125%

Hydrangea Handbag

The clusters of flowers on the sides of this bag are made with one large piece of fabric. It is stitched with the shapes of individual flowers, creating the illusion of many fabric pieces. Enhance the flower centers with crystals, machine details, or bead embellishment. The fully-lined bag is one piece of fabric, artfully shaped by the way it's constructed.

Refer to *Fabrics* and to *Threads* (page 5); to *Interfacing* and to *Crystals* (page 6); to *Stitching* (page 7); to *Stitching Shapes* (page 9); to *Light Box* (page 11); and to *Fusible Web* (page 12) before beginning. Test thread colors, stitch lengths, and stitch widths on fabric scraps.

When using any fusible product, always follow the manufacturer's instructions.

Materials

- Tracing paper, 18" × 24" (45.7 × 61 cm)
- Light- or medium-weight fusible interfacing, 1 yd. (0.9 m)
- Bag fabric, ½ yd. (0.5 m)
- Lining fabric, ½ yd. (0.5 m)
- Light box
- Paper-backed fusible web, 12" (30.5 cm)
- Flower fabric, hand-dyed, fat quarter

- Threads
- Forty-six crystals, 5 mm
- Button, ¾" (1.9 cm) or 1" (2.5 cm)

1 Enlarge the bag and flower outlines (page 63) by 200 percent, then trace the patterns onto the tracing paper.

2 Fold the bag and lining fabrics and the interfacing in half. Place the bag pattern on each in turn, positioning the bag handle at the fold, and cut out. Trim the seams on the interfacing to ¼" (6 mm). Cut two 1¾" × 3" (4.5 × 7.6 cm) pieces of outer fabric for the button tabs.

3 Mark the darts and the side point on the interfacing and on the lining. Adhere the interfacing to the wrong side of the bag fabric.

4 Trace the outline of the flower bunch pattern onto tracing paper. Trace the pattern onto the fusible web using a light box. Turn the pattern over and trace the outline again, for the second flower bunch. Adhere both pieces of fusible web to the wrong side of the flower fabric, leaving the paper-backing intact. Cut the patterns out along the traced lines.

5 Use the flower pattern and the light box to trace the individual flower shapes onto the

right side of the flower fabric. The lines will be hidden when you stitch over them. Fuse the flower fabrics to the bag fabric, referring to the pattern for placement.

6 Use a narrow zigzag stitch to outline the individual flowers, decreasing the width of the zigzag as it approaches the flower center. The bag shown has cotton, rayon, and polyester threads in a variety of colors to add interest to the flowers. Zigzag stitch each flower individually and change the thread color as often as desired.

Note: Some of the flowers overlap. Stitch the underneath flowers first, so the stitching on the top flowers will cover the ends and give the illusion of depth. Pull all threads to the back, knot, and trim.

7 Apply the crystals to create the flower centers.

8 Stitch the button tab, right sides together, with ¼" (6 mm) seams, leaving one end open for turning. Turn, then press. Make a buttonhole on the closed end of the tab.

Continued ⋮▸

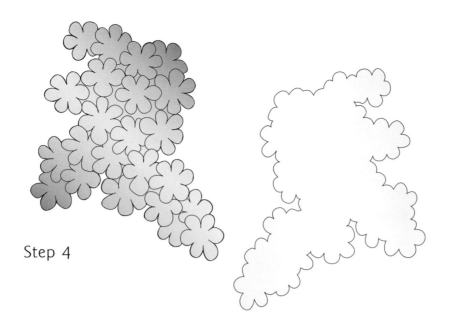

Step 4

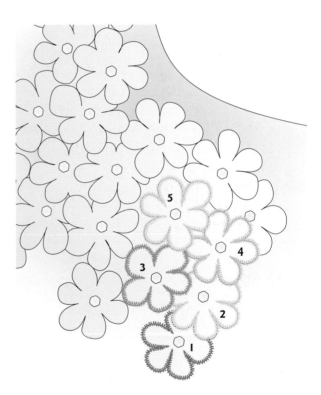

Step 6

9 To construct the bag, use a ½" (1.3 cm) seam for all stitching. Stitch the darts on the wrong side of the fabric. Stitch the center seams, right sides together, and press open. Stitch the bag bottom, right sides together. Fold under ½" (1.3 cm) along the top edge of the bag and handle. Clip into the seam allowance on the curves as needed. Press the edge. Repeat the procedure for the lining.

10 Pin the bag and the lining together, matching the edges carefully. Pin the tab into the back of the bag at the center seam. Topstitch the outer bag and lining together very close to the edge.

11 Sew the button to the front of the bag at the center seam.

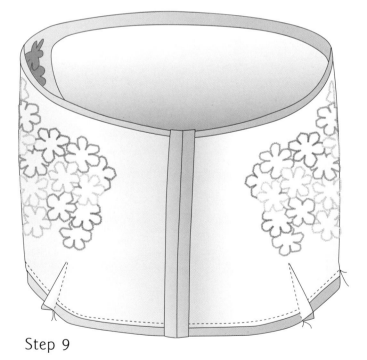

Step 9

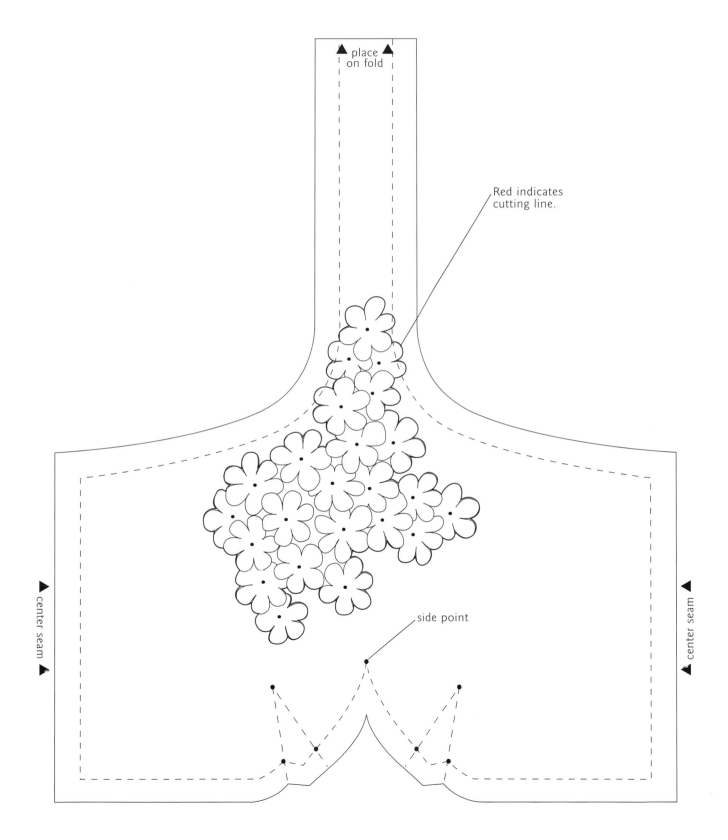

place on fold

Red indicates cutting line.

center seam

center seam

side point

Jewelry Tri-Tote

Whether you use it on the road or at home, this fold-over jewelry bag protects precious jewelry in its zippered inner pockets and handy snap-fastened ring holder. "Sew" a field of colorful flowers, for this motif lends itself to unlimited color choices.

The petal and leaf patterns are reversed. You will transfer them to fusible web, then fuse them to the wrong side of the fabrics. When cut out, they will appear in the right orientation.

Refer to *Fabrics* and to *Threads* (page 5); to *Aerosol Spray Baste*, to *Removable Stabilizers*, to *Even Feed or Walking Machine Foot* and to *Light Box* (page 6); to *Stitching* (page 7); to *Stitching Shapes* (page 9); and to *Fusible Web* (page 12) before beginning. Test thread colors, stitch lengths, and stitch widths on fabric scraps.

When using any fusible product, always follow the manufacturer's instructions.

Materials

- Paper-backed light-weight fusible web, 8" × 11" (20.3 × 27.9 cm)
- Three petal fabrics, related colors, 4" (10.2 cm) square
- Leaf fabric, 6" (15.2 cm) square
- Bag/lining fabric, ¼ yd. (0.2 m)
- Thin batting, 7" × 9" (17.8 × 22.9 cm)
- Light box
- Aerosol spray baste

- Removable stabilizer, 8" × 10" (20.3 × 25.4 cm)
- Threads
- Even feed or walking machine foot (optional)
- Twelve inches (30.5 cm) ribbon, ¼" (6 mm) wide
- Two zippers, 7" (17.8 cm)
- Snap

Note: This bag could be made with cotton or special-occasion fabrics.

1 Trace the petal and leaf patterns (page 71) onto tracing paper and cut them out. Draw around the patterns on the fusible web paper-backing. Adhere the web to the wrong side of the appropriate fabrics, leaving the backing intact. Cut the patterns out along the traced lines.

2 From the bag fabric, cut one 6½" × 8½" (16.5 × 21.6 cm) piece for the front, two 2" × 6½" (5.1 × 16.5 cm) pieces for pocket A, two 3½" × 6½" (8.9 × 16.5 cm) pieces for pocket B, one 2" × 5½" (5.1 × 14 cm) piece and one 2" (5.1 cm) square for the ring holder. From both the batting and the lining fabric, cut one 6½" × 8½" (16.5 × 21.6 cm) piece.

3 Trace the complete appliqué motif (page 69) onto tracing paper. Place the traced pattern, then the front fabric right side up, on the light box. Trace the pattern with a chalk pencil.

4 Adhere the leaves to the front fabric. Spritz spray baste on one side of the removable stabilizer. Adhere the stabilizer to the wrong side of the front fabric. Be sure the stabilizer is under all the stitching areas. Zigzag stitch the edges of all the leaves. Pull all the threads to the back, knot, and trim. Use a wide setting and the zigzag rope stitch to create the stem.

5 Assemble the flower and the bud following the numerical order on the pattern (page 69). Zigzag stitch only the petal edges that show, and along the false petal stitch line. Create a stamen with a straight stitch, and a pollen cap with a varied-width zigzag stitch, using a shiny thread. Remove the stabilizer.

6 Pin the batting to the wrong side of the front fabric. Stitch around the inner petals, then the outer petals, and then the leaves and stem, using a straight stitch and a thread color darker than each design element's zigzagged thread. Baste the outer edges of the front fabric within the seam allowance to hold the layers together. Trim the batting flush with the front fabric.

Note: This step is easiest when using a walking or even feed machine foot to quilt the design elements.

Continued ⁝

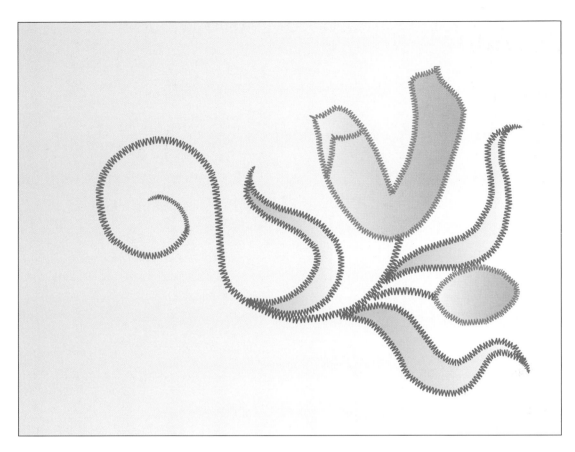

Step 5

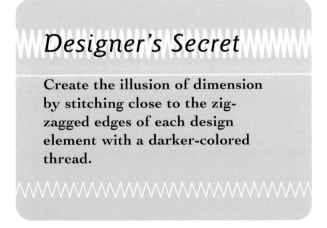

Designer's Secret

Create the illusion of dimension by stitching close to the zig-zagged edges of each design element with a darker-colored thread.

7 Cut the ribbon into two equal halves. Fold one piece in half and baste to the center of a short side of the fabric front. Repeat with the other piece on the other short side.

8 **Note:** The zippers are longer than the pockets. Start stitching at the top of the zipper; the excess will be trimmed.

Fold one piece of pocket A fabric in half lengthwise, wrong sides together, and press.

Lay the folded edge of pocket A along the outside of a zipper and topstitch to the zipper. Fold both long ends of one pocket B fabric ½" (1.3 cm) to the wrong side and press. Place the pocket on the zipper and topstitch to the zipper. Repeat the procedure with the other zipper and pocket fabrics.

Continued ⋮➤

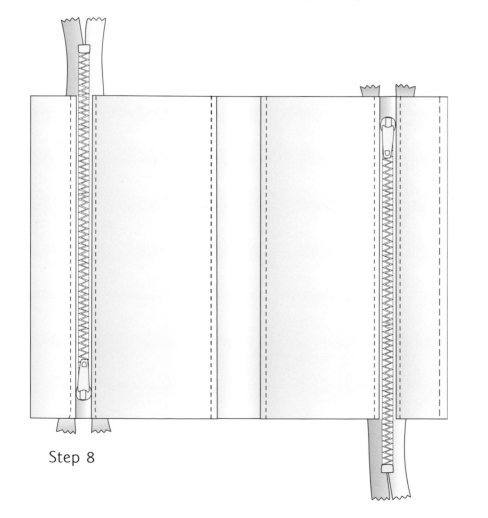

Step 8

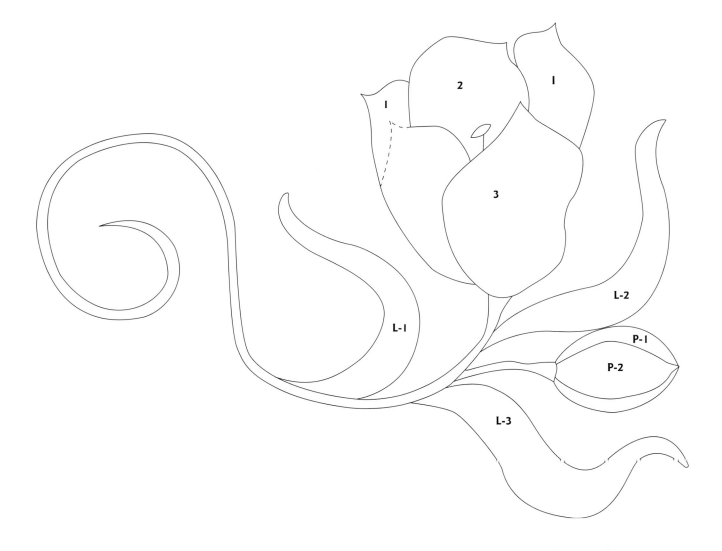

9 Lay the pockets on the lining, right sides up. Topstitch the pocket bottom edges to the lining. Machine baste the pocket outer edges to the lining, within the seam allowance.

10 Fold the ring holder fabric pieces in half lengthwise, right sides together, and stitch with ¼" (6 mm) seams, leaving one short end open for turning. Clip the corners, turn, and press. Place both sections on the center "spine" of the lining with each open end on a lining edge. Machine baste the ring-holder pieces to the lining.

11 Pin the bag front to the lining, right sides together, and stitch with ¼" (6 mm) seams, leaving one short end open for turning. Trim the zippers. Clip the corners, turn, and handstitch the opening closed. Press lightly. Handstitch the ball side of the snap under the end of the long section of the ring holder, and the socket side to the top of the short section, at the end.

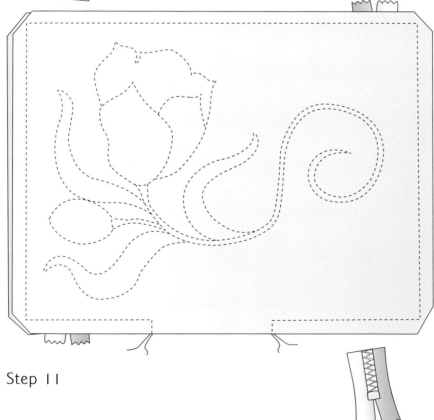

Step 11

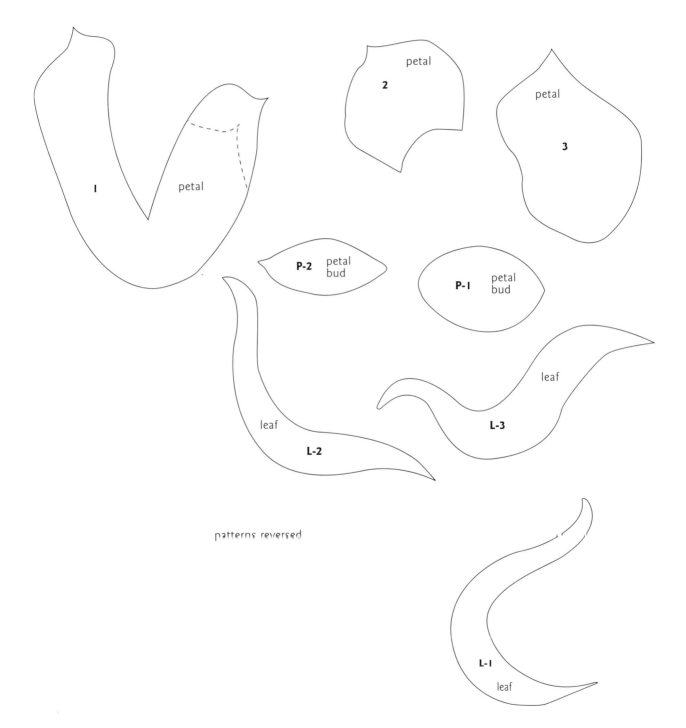

1 petal

2 petal

3 petal

P-2 petal bud

P-1 petal bud

leaf L-2

leaf L-3

patterns reversed

L-1 leaf

Bluebells
Journal Cover

Transform a small blank book into an exquisite gift when you cover it with a bluebell and bead embellished cover. Stuffing the diminutive flowers and the bud adds dimension and realism to the design.

The leaf patterns are reversed. You will transfer them to freezer paper, then fuse them to the wrong side of the fabric. When cut out, they will appear in the right orientation.

Refer to *Fabrics* and to *Threads* (page 5); to *Removable Stabilizers* (page 6); to *Stitching* (page 7); to *Stitching Shapes* (page 9); to *Freezer Paper* (page 12); and to *Beading* (page 13) before beginning. Test thread colors, stitch lengths, and stitch widths on fabric scraps.

Materials

Freezer paper, 6" (15.2 cm) square

Cover fabric, ¼ yd. (0.2 m)

Lining/pocket fabric, ¼ yd. (0.2 m)

Leaf fabric, 7" (17.8 cm) square

Mini iron for pressing small items (optional)

Flower fabric, 6" (15.2 cm) square

Dime (coin)

Bud fabric, 1" (2.5 cm) square

Threads

Twenty-four seed beads, black

Beading needle

Beading thread

Removable stabilizer, 6" (15.2 cm) square

Fiberfill

Blank journal, approximately 6" × 8" (15.2 × 20.3 cm)

Note: Covering a larger or smaller journal requires an adjustment to the amount of fabric needed. To measure the length of fabric needed for the cover, run your tape measure from the bottom of the back around the spine to the bottom of the front and add ¾" (1.9 cm). To find the length of the inner pockets, measure the front and add 1" (2.5 cm). The lining length is 1" (2.5 cm) shorter than the length of the front. Measure across the front and add ¾" (1.9 cm) for the width of the cover, lining, and each pocket.

1 Enlarge the entire design motif (page 75) by 125 percent. Trace the motif onto tracing paper and the leaf and flower patterns onto the dull side of the freezer paper.

2 Cut one cover piece 6¾" × 19⅛" (17.2 × 48.6 cm), one lining piece 6¾" × 7" (17.2 × 17.8 cm), and two pieces for the inner pockets 6¾" × 9" (17.2 × 22.9 cm).

3 Pin the tracing paper to the right side of the front cover fabric. Straight stitch the stem lines through the paper and the fabric. Pull the threads to the back, knot, and trim. Remove the tracing paper.

4 Cut out the leaf and flower patterns. Iron the freezer paper to the wrong side of the leaf and flower fabrics. Cut around the patterns, allowing a scant ¼" (6 mm) seam allowance. Fold the seam allowance under and press in place (a standard iron works for this, but a mini iron is easier to use). Clip the seam allowance as needed to allow the curves to lie flat. Remove the freezer paper. Press the pieces again.

5 To make the bud, place a dime on the wrong side of the bud fabric. Draw around the dime with a pencil; then cut along the line. Handstitch a running stitch very close to the edge of the circle. Gently pull the thread to gather the edges of the fabric in toward the center. Tie the thread. Press the bud.

6 Place, then pin, the bud and flowers on the cover, using the stitched stem line as a placement guide. Topstitch the bud and flowers close to the edge with a straight stitch and matching thread. Sew a line of four beads, and one bead to either side of the line, at the center of each flower's mouth. Pull all the threads to the back, knot, and trim.

7 Place, then pin, the leaves on the cover. Topstitch the leaves close to the edge, and the leaf veins with a straight stitch and contrasting thread. Pull all the threads to the back, knot, and trim. Place removable stabilizer under the cover fabric and zigzag stitch the stems. Remove the stabilizer.

8 To stuff the flowers and the bud, cut a small slit from the wrong side into the cover fabric behind the flowers and bud. Push the desired amount of stuffing into the flowers or bud.

Continued ⸖

9 Fold the pockets lengthwise, wrong sides together, and press. Place the cover right side up and lay the inner pockets on each end with the folded edge toward the center. Center the lining, wrong side up, in the middle of the cover. Pin the layers together and stitch around all the edges with a ¼" (6 mm) seam. Clip the corners, turn, and press. Put the cover on the journal.

ENLARGE 125%

Step 4

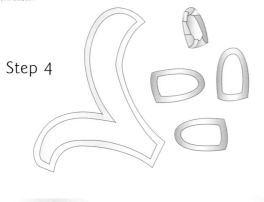

Step 7

Step 9

patterns reversed

ENLARGE 125%

Designer's Secret

When zigzag stitching stems, make the smaller branches look like they are growing out of the larger stem by first stitching the smaller branches and connecting the larger stem to look natural. Stitch the smaller branches with a narrower stitch than the main stem.

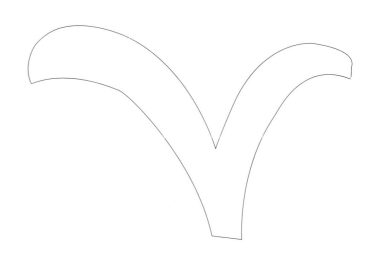

Dainties and Delicates Bag

Feminine fashion fabrics form a delicate bag to keep pretty lingerie or hose safely stored. A cluster of beads and the sparkle of opalescent monofilament thread add a touch of shimmering elegance.

Refer to *Fabrics* and to *Threads* (page 5); to *Aerosol Spray Baste* (page 6); to *Stitching* (page 7); to *Stitching Shapes* (page 9); to *Removable Stabilizers* (page 11); to *Fusible Web* (page 12); and to *Beading* (page 13) before beginning. Test thread colors, stitch lengths, and stitch widths on fabric scraps.

When using any fusible product, always follow the manufacturer's instructions.

Materials

- Paper-backed fusible web, 6" (15.2 cm) square

- Leaf fabric, 6" (15.2 cm) square

- One-third yd. (0.3 m) bag fabric, special occasion, 44" (111.8 cm) or wider

- Aerosol spray baste

- Removable stabilizer, 8" (20.3 cm) square

- Threads, to match fabric and opalescent monofilament

- Beads, assorted colors, 4 mm

- Beading needle

- Beading thread

- Thirty-six inches (91.4 cm) ribbon, ⅛" (3 mm) wide

1 Trace the outline of the leaf pattern (page 81) onto tracing paper and cut it out. Draw around the pattern on the fusible web paper-backing. Adhere the web to the wrong side of the leaf fabric, leaving the backing intact. Cut the pattern out along the traced lines.

2 Trace the bag pattern (page 81) onto tracing paper. Fold the bag fabric and use the pattern to cut two bags. Also cut a 2¾" × 40½" (7 × 102.9 cm) gusset and two 8¼" × 1" (21 × 2.5 cm) ribbon holders.

3 Mark the bag fabric on both edges of the fold line and on the centerpoints. Fold the gusset and mark on both edges at the fold. Measure in from each end of the gusset 10¼" (26 cm) and mark on both edges.

4 Adhere the leaf to the right side of the bag. Spritz spray baste on one side of the removable stabilizer. Adhere the stabilizer to the wrong side of the bag fabric, creating a sandwich of leaf, bag fabric, and stabilizer. Be sure the stabilizer is under all stitching areas. Use a chalk pencil to mark the stitching lines on the leaf. Zigzag stitch the leaf with a plain-colored thread, using a narrower stitch at the points. Overstitch with opalescent monofilament thread in the same manner. Pull all threads to the back, knot, and trim. Remove the stabilizer. Handstitch the beads on the leaf.

5 Stitch the short ends of the gusset, right sides together, using a ¼" (6 mm) seam to form a circle. Press the seam open.

6 Pin the gusset to the bag, right sides together, matching all marks. Stitch the gusset to the bag fabric with the leaf appliqué, using a ¼" (6 mm) seam. Repeat for the other side, leaving an opening for turning. Turn, then press lightly. Handstitch the opening closed. Fold the fabric in half to form a bag.

Continued ⋗

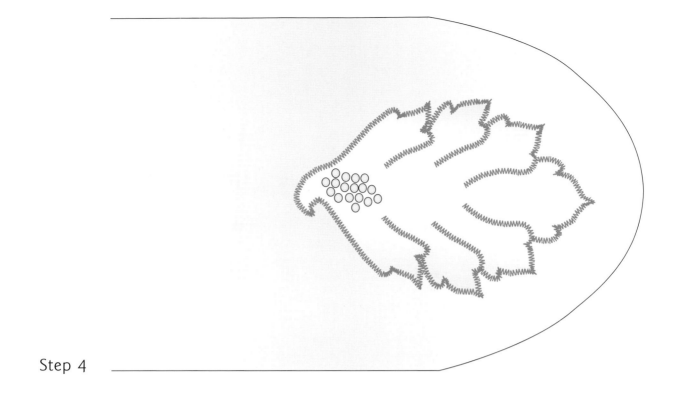

Step 4

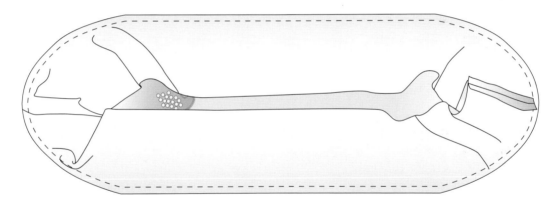

Step 6

Designer's Secret

To attach a straight edge
smoothly to a curved edge, first
mark the join areas and pin
together at the marks, clipping
the straight edge as needed,
from the outside edge almost
into the seamline.

7 Fold under the long edges of the ribbon holders ¼" (6 mm) and press. Fold under the ends of the ribbon holders ¼" (6 mm) and press. Pin the ribbon holders to the bag, 1" (2.5 cm) down from the fold, with the ends of each holder on the gussets (there will be a space between the ends of the ribbon holders). Stitch in place.

8 Cut the ribbon in half. Thread one ribbon through both ribbon holders. Repeat with the other ribbon, threading in the opposite direction. Trim to the desired length and knot.

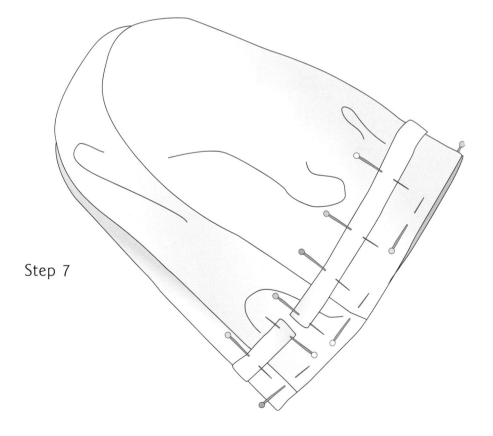

Step 7

▲ place on fold ▲

Pentagon Box

Create this sophisticated, stained-glass-effect box for storing special treasures. A solid satin stitch done in rayon thread gives dimension to this appliqué. Beaded accents add sparkle and interest.

Refer to *Fabrics* and to *Threads* (page 5); to *Aerosol Spray Baste*, to *Interfacing*, and to *Light Box* (page 6); to *Stitching* (page 7); to *Stitching Shapes* (page 9); to *Fusible Web* (page 12); and to *Beading* (page 13) before beginning. Test thread colors, stitch lengths, and stitch widths on fabric scraps.

When using any fusible product, always follow the manufacturer's instructions.

Materials

- Tracing paper, 18" × 24" (45.7 × 61 cm)
- Outer box fabric, ½ yd. (0.5 m)
- Lining fabric, ½ yd. (0.5 m)
- Double-sided stiff fusible interfacing, 12" × 24" (30.5 × 61 cm)
- Paper-backed fusible web, 8" (20.3 cm) square
- Berry fabric, 4" (10.2 cm) square
- Leaf fabric, 6" (15.2 cm) square
- Light box

- Appliqué circle fabric, 8" (20.3 cm) square
- Medium-weight fusible interfacing, 6" (15.2 cm) square
- Threads
- Aerosol spray baste
- Seed beads, dark green
- Beading thread
- Beading needle

1 Enlarge the box patterns (page 87), by 200 percent. Draw a line vertically down the center of a sheet of tracing paper. Place the line along the midline of the box top pattern, and trace all the lines. Turn the paper over, match the center lines, and trace all the lines to develop the complete pattern. Cut it out.

2 The outer pattern line indicates the outer fabric; the second line indicates the lining; and the inner line indicates the interfacing. Only one tracing is necessary if you cut the material in the order given. Position, then pin, the pattern on the outer fabric, and cut it out. Repeat on the lining fabric, then on the interfacing. Repeat steps 1 and 2 for the box base.

3 Trace the outline of one berry and the leaf patterns (page 86) onto tracing paper and cut them out. On the fusible web paper-backing, draw around the berry pattern eight times; reverse the leaf patterns and draw around them. Rough cut the patterns apart. Adhere the web to the wrong side of the appropriate fabrics, leaving the backing intact. Cut the patterns out along the traced lines.

4 Use a light box to trace the circle shape and the inner design lines (page 86) onto the right side of the appliqué circle fabric with a chalk or other pencil. These lines will be stitched over. Adhere the leaves and berries to the circle, guided by the chalked lines. Adhere the medium-weight fusible interfacing to the wrong side of the circle. Cut the circle out along the traced line.

5 Zigzag stitch all the inner design elements using a medium-width stitch; overstitch with a slightly wider stitch.

6 Adhere the wrong side of the outer fabric to the double-sided fusible interfacing. Carefully position the appliqué circle on the right side of the outer fabric, in the center, and spray baste to attach. Zigzag stitch around the circle using a wide zigzag stitch; overstitch with a slightly wider stitch. Handstitch the beads along the center vein of each leaf.

7 Center the lining on the wrong side of the outer fabric, over the interfacing, and fuse.

Continued ⋗

Step 4

Step 6

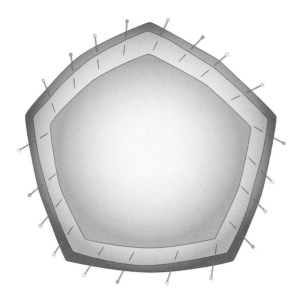

Step 9

8 Fold one set of adjacent corner lines together, matching the interfacing edges, right sides of the outer fabric together, and pin. Stitch along the edge of the interfacing on the inside of the box. This will look like a dart. Repeat for all corners.

9 Finish the edge of the box top by folding the outer fabric to the inside along the top of the interfacing. Fold again to cover the raw edge, and pin. Topstitch the folded edge in place. Press the box top to square the shape.

10 Adhere the wrong side of the outer fabric to the double-sided fusible interfacing; then repeat steps 7 to 9 to construct the box base.

Pentagon Box Pattern
ACTUAL SIZE

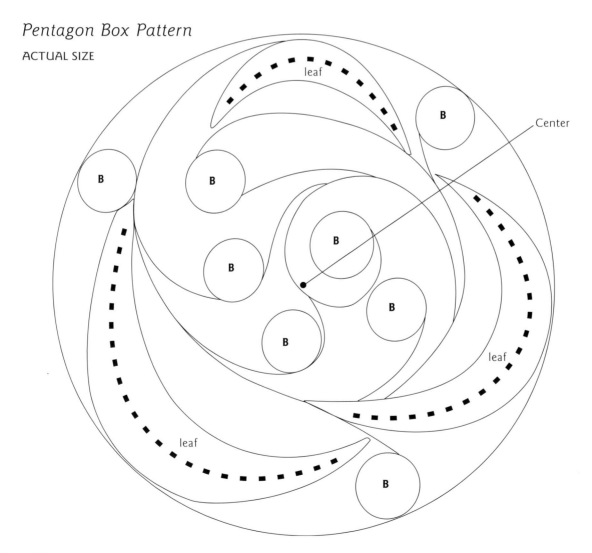

▲ Place on fold ▲

box top

▲ Place on fold ▲

box base

KEY TO STITCHES & FOLDING

————————	outerfabric
— — — — — ·	lining
· · · · · · · · · · ·	stiff interfacing
· — · — · — ·	combination
··· —— ··· —— ···	folding line

Pink Lily Scarf

Delicate and chic, this scarf becomes the focal point of any ensemble. A dangle of beads adds sparkle and movement to catch the fashionable eye.

Refer to *Fabrics* and to *Threads* (page 5); to *Aerosol Spray Baste,* to *Removable Stabilizers,* and to *Light Box* (page 6); to *Stitching* (page 7); to *Stitching Shapes* (page 9); and to *Beading* (page 13) before beginning. Test thread colors, stitch lengths, and stitch widths on fabric scraps.

Materials

- Georgette or chiffon for scarf, 2 yd. (1.8 m)
- Water-soluble stabilizer, 6" × 8" (15.2 × 20.3 cm)
- Light box
- Aerosol spray baste
- Two flower fabrics, related color, soft fashion, 6" × 9" (15.2 × 22.9 cm)
- Threads

- Aurora Borealis crystal beads, 6 mm, 4 mm, 3 mm
- Beading thread
- Beading needle

Note: Georgette and chiffon come in easy-care polyester, with the soft hand perfect for a scarf. Cut the fabric lengthwise to achieve the proper drape. Two yards (1.8 m) of fabric make two or three scarves, depending on width.

1 Cut two scarf pieces 72" × 8" (182.9 × 20.3 cm). **Note:** The seams for the scarf are ½" (1.3 cm) for ease of stitching, and they can be trimmed to ¼" (6 mm) before turning.

2 Trace the lily top and bottom patterns (page 93) onto tracing paper. Trace the entire design motif (page 92), including the center line, onto the removable stabilizer using a light box and a pencil. Spritz spray baste on the patterned side of the removable stabilizer. Adhere the stabilizer to the wrong side of the scarf fabric. Make sure the stabilizer is under all the stitching areas.

3 Lay the lily bottom pattern on the right side of the appropriate fabric. Stabilize the fabric for the lily bottom by making a sandwich of pattern, fabric, and scrap paper; then pin together and cut along the pattern lines. Repeat with the pattern and fabric for the lily top.

4 Remove the pattern and the scrap paper from both fabric pieces. Spritz spray baste on the wrong side of the lily bottom and place it on the right side of the scarf, using the lines on the stabilizer as a guide. Zigzag stitch the lily bottom petal areas. Pull the threads to the back, knot, and trim.

5 Spritz spray baste on the wrong side of the lily top and place it on the right side of the scarf, using the lines on the stabilizer as a guide. Mark the center petal stitching lines with a chalk pencil. First stitch the lily top along all the lines indicated with red (refer to illustration), then along all the lines indicated with blue, making sure the ends of the red stitch lines are covered. The zigzag stitching at the tips should be very narrow. Zigzag stitch the stem.

Continued ⋮

Designer's Secret

Lines on the stabilizer can be seen through light-colored fabric. Trace the pattern onto the stabilizer, put it under the fabric, and you will easily see where to place the appliqué pieces.

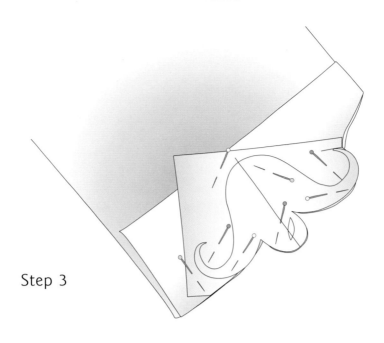

Step 3

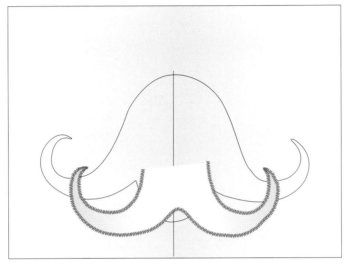

Step 4

KEY TO STITCHING ORDER

———— Red- stitch first

———— Blue- stitch second

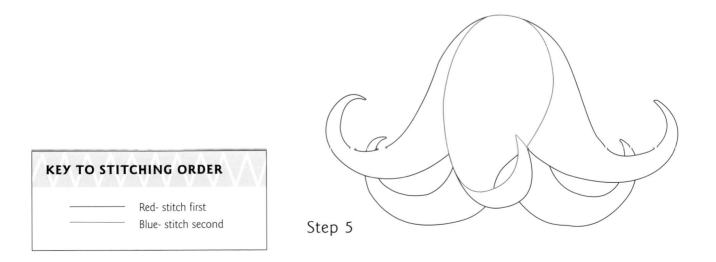

Step 5

6 Pull off all the stabilizer that can be removed; then follow the manufacturer's instructions to remove the remaining stabilizer with water. Allow the fabric to dry.

7 Lay the scarf pieces right sides together and pin. Stitch the pieces together using a ½" (1.3 cm) seam, leaving an opening for turning. Follow the outline of the lily pattern on the appliqué end of the scarf when stitching and trimming—the end opposite the lily remains square. Trim the seams to ¼" (6 mm) and clip the lily's indentation and curves. Turn the scarf and handstitch the opening closed. Press lightly.

8 Stitch into the scarf with the beading needle to secure the thread. Thread the beads on the beading thread in the desired pattern, ending with a small bead. Pass by the small bead and return the thread through all the other beads, securing the thread in the scarf. Repeat four more times.

Pink Lily Scarf Pattern
ACTUAL SIZE

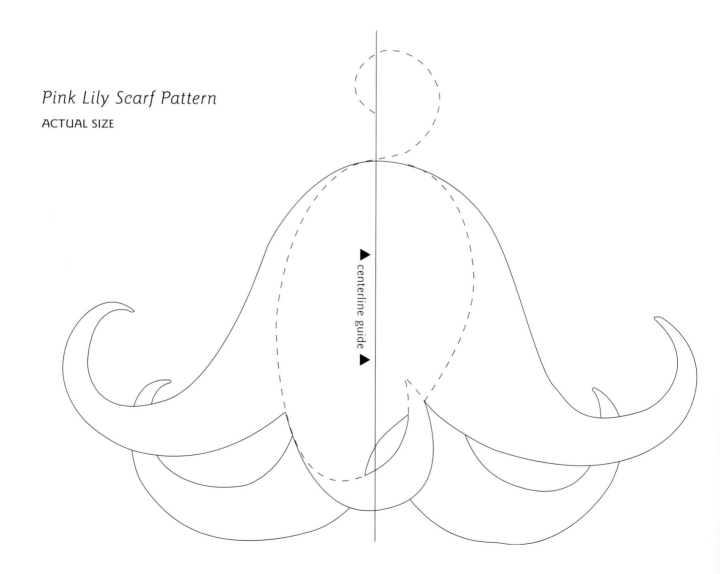

centerline guide

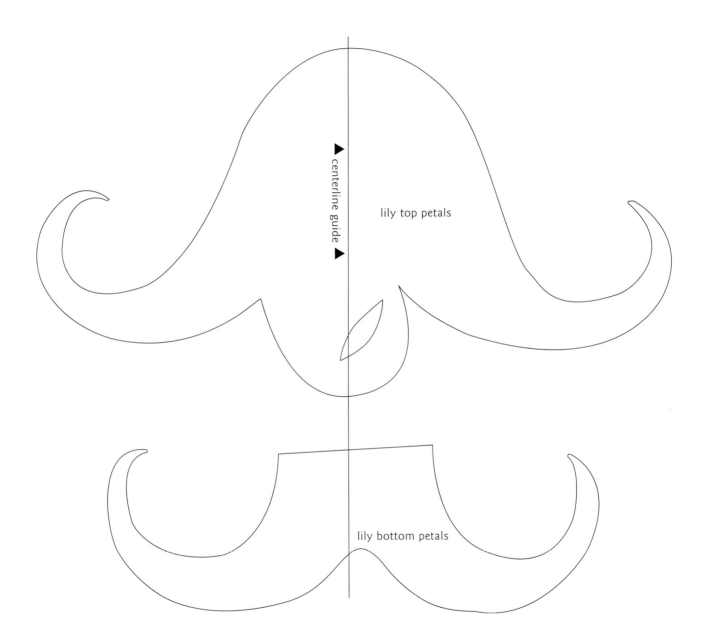

centerline guide

lily top petals

lily bottom petals

Black-Eyed Susan Planner Cover

This cheery, happy, black-eyed Susan cover for the pocket planner so many of us carry offers a fun way to use embellished appliqué techniques to create a unique gift. Adapt the design for a matching checkbook cover.

The flower and leaf patterns are reversed. You will transfer them to fusible web, then fuse them to the wrong side of the fabrics. When cut out, they will appear in the right orientation.

Refer to *Threads* and to *Fabrics* (page 5); to *Aerosol Spray Baste*, to *Removable Stabilizers* and to *Crystals* (page 6); to *Pattern Placement Using a Motif Cutout* and to *Stitching* (page 7); to *Stitching Shapes* (page 9); to *Fusible Web* (page 12) before beginning. Test thread colors, stitch lengths, and stitch widths on fabric scraps.

When using any fusible product, always follow the manufacturer's instructions.

Materials

Paper-backed light-weight fusible web, 8" × 11" (20.3 × 27.9 cm)

Three flower fabrics, 4" (10.2 cm) square each

Flower center fabric, 2" (5.1 cm) square

Leaf fabric, 4" (10.2 cm) square

Cover/lining fabric, fat quarter

Aerosol spray baste

Removable stabilizer, 8" × 10" (20.3 × 25.4 cm)

Threads

Nine crystals, 2 mm

Planner, 7⅝" × 6½" (19.4 × 16.5 cm)

Note: Covering a larger or smaller planner requires an adjustment to the amount of fabric needed. To measure the width of fabric needed for the cover, run your tape measure across the open planner from the back edge to the front edge and add ¾" (1.9 cm). To find the width of the inner pockets, measure the front and add 1" (2.5 cm). This is slightly larger than the measurement given for the pockets on this planner cover. The lining width is 4" (10.2 cm) narrower than the width of the front. Measure the length of the front and add ¾" (1.9 cm) for the length of the cover, lining, and each pocket.

1 Trace the entire design motif (page 98) onto tracing paper. Trace the flower and leaf patterns (page 99) onto tracing paper and cut them out. Draw around each pattern on the fusible web paper-backing. Rough cut the patterns apart. Adhere the web to the wrong side of the appropriate fabrics, leaving the backing intact. Cut the patterns out along the traced lines.

2 Cut one cover piece 8⅜" × 7¼" (21.3 × 18.4 cm), one lining piece 4⅜" × 7¼" (11.1 × 18.4 cm), and two inner pocket pieces 6" × 7¼" (15.2 × 18.4 cm).

3 Create a placement guide by cutting around the traced motif along the outer flower and leaf edges. Position the cutout on the right side of the cover fabric between the seam allowances, and draw around the shape with a chalk pencil. Remove the traced pattern.

4 Spritz spray baste on one side of the removable stabilizer. Adhere the stabilizer to the wrong side of the cover fabric under the stitching area.

5 Position, adhere, and then zigzag stitch the leaves, using a narrow width. Zigzag stitch the stem using a wider stitch. Repeat the positioning, adhering, and stitching with flower pattern 1. Repeat with flower pattern 2 and add straight stitching following the shape of the petals. Repeat with flower pattern 3 and then the center. Pull all threads to the back, knot, and trim. Remove the stabilizer.

Continued ⫶

Step 3

Step 5

Designer's Secret

To create the illusion of layers when stitching, start with the rearmost layer and stitch a few stitches into the area to be covered by the next layer. The stitching on subsequent layers will overlap the layers underneath.

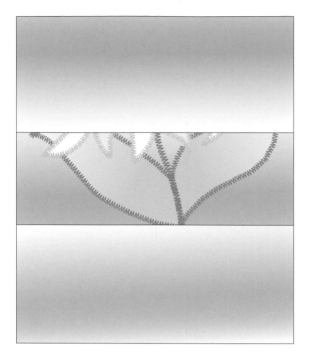

Step 6

6 Fold the pockets lengthwise, wrong sides together, and press. Place the cover right side up and lay the inner pockets on each end, with the folded edge toward the center. Center the lining, wrong side up, in the middle of the cover. Pin the layers together and stitch around all the edges with a ¼" (6 mm) seam. Clip the corners, turn, and press.

7 Adhere the crystals to the flower center. Put the cover on the planner.

Black-Eyed Susan Planner Cover Pattern

ACTUAL SIZE

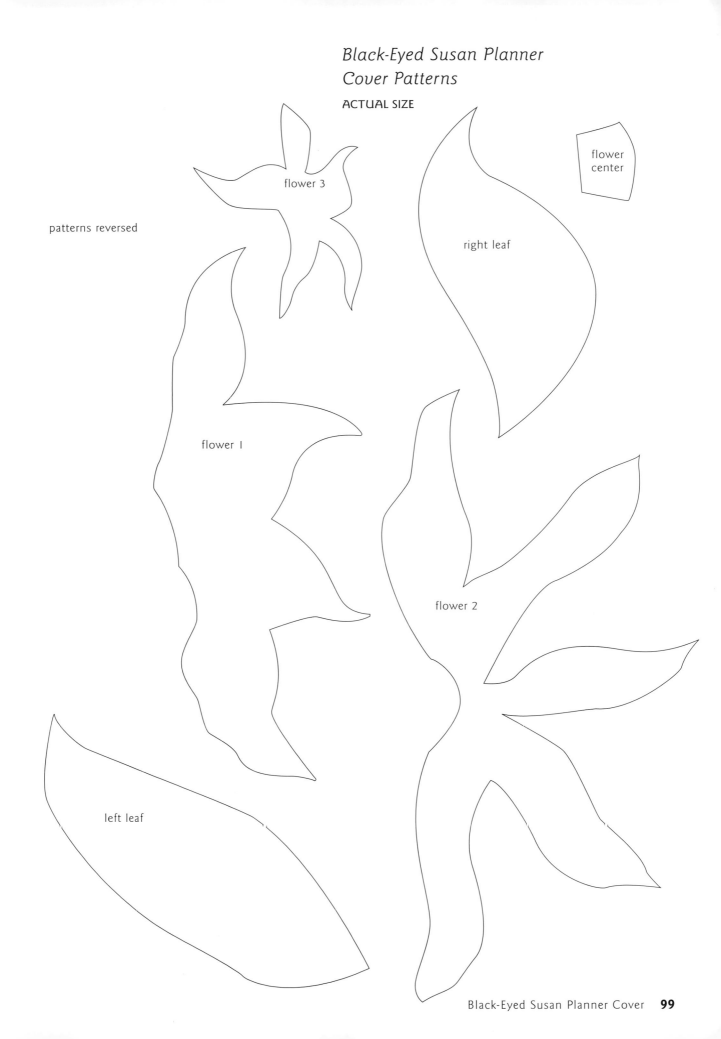

*Black-Eyed Susan Planner
Cover Patterns*

ACTUAL SIZE

flower 3

flower center

right leaf

patterns reversed

flower 1

flower 2

left leaf

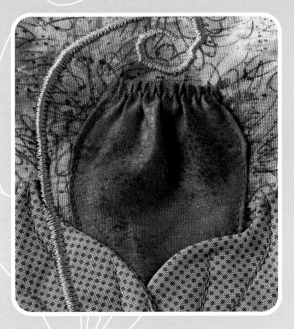

Tiny Treasures Sewing Necklace

This necklace holds all a hand sewer's tools. A thimble hides in the front flower, a small scissors and spool of thread nestle in an inner pocket, and a wool needle-keep holds pins and needles.

Refer to *Fabrics* and to *Threads* (page 5); to *Interfacing* and to *Light Box* (page 6); to *Pattern Placement Using a Motif Cutout* and to *Stitching* (page 7); to *Stitching Shapes* (page 9); and to *Beading* (page 13) before beginning. Test thread colors, stitch lengths, and stitch widths on fabric scraps.

When using any fusible product, always follow the manufacturer's instructions.

Materials

- Felted wool, 4" (10.2 cm) square
- Thimble pocket fabric, 4" (10.2 cm) square
- Scissors pocket fabric, 12" × 5" (30.5 × 12.7 cm)
- Leaf fabric, 4" × 8" (10.2 × 20.3 cm)
- Cover fabric, 12" × 5" (30.5 × 12.7 cm)
- Lining fabric, 12" × 5" (30.5 × 12.7 cm)
- Light-weight fusible interfacing, 5" × 7" (12.7 × 17.8 cm)

- Light box
- Four inches (10.2 cm) elastic, ¼" (6 mm) wide
- Threads
- Glass beads, 6 mm
- Beading thread
- Beading needle

1 Trace all the sewing necklace patterns (pages 104 and 105) onto tracing paper, cut them out, and pin them to the appropriate fabrics. Cut one needle page from the felted wool. Cut out one thimble pocket, one scissors pocket, two right and two left leaves, one cover and one lining. Trace the cover/lining pattern from the fold line to the point, and use it to cut one piece of interfacing and trim the point.

2 Trace the entire design motif (page 103) onto tracing paper. Use a light box and chalk pencil to trace the placement of the thimble pocket, the leaves, and the stem onto the right side of the front of the cover.

3 Fuse the interfacing to the wrong side of the cover, under the traced pattern.

4 Fold the top of the thimble pocket to the wrong side ½" (1.3 cm). Put the elastic under the folded edge, pull it taut, then stitch with a zigzag. Trim extra elastic away. Fold under the seam allowance ¼" (6 mm) and press. Pin the pocket in place on the cover. Topstitch with straight machine stitching next to the edge.

5 Pin the leaves right sides together and stitch as indicated on the pattern. Turn and press. Pin the right leaf on the cover, then stitch leaf veins through all the layers. Pin the left leaf on the cover, stitch the edge where it overlaps the right leaf, and then stitch the vein lines through all the layers. Pull all threads to the back, knot, and trim. Create the stem with a zigzag stitch.

6 Stitch the needle page on the lining ½" (1.3 cm) down from the fold line.

7 Lay the lining right side up. Fold the scissors pocket in half, wrong sides together. Place the folded scissors pocket on the lining, opposite the needle page. Place the cover, wrong side up, on top of the lining, with the front over the needle page. Pin the layers together and stitch, leaving an opening for turning. Trim the points, turn, and press.

8 Cut a thread long enough for the necklace. Stitch the thread inside the bag on the left corner to secure it, and pull the thread through. Add the beads in the pattern desired. Stitch the necklace end to the inside right of the bag and secure. Blindstitch the opening closed.

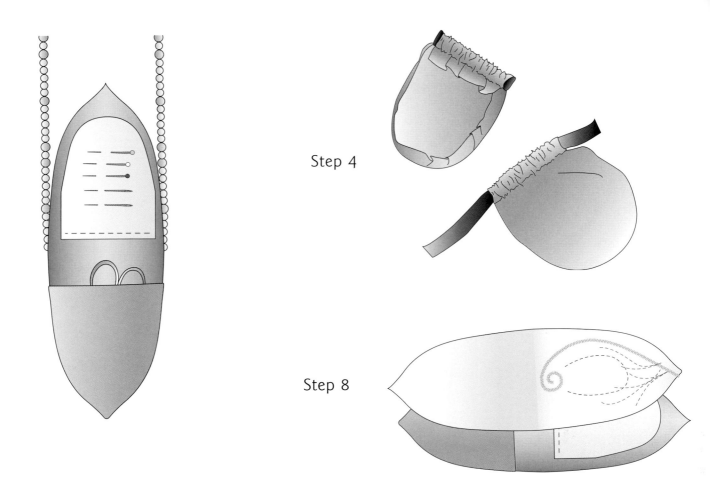

Step 4

Step 8

Tiny Treasures
Sewing Necklace
Entire Motif Pattern
ACTUAL SIZE

Tiny Treasures Sewing
Necklace Patterns
ACTUAL SIZE

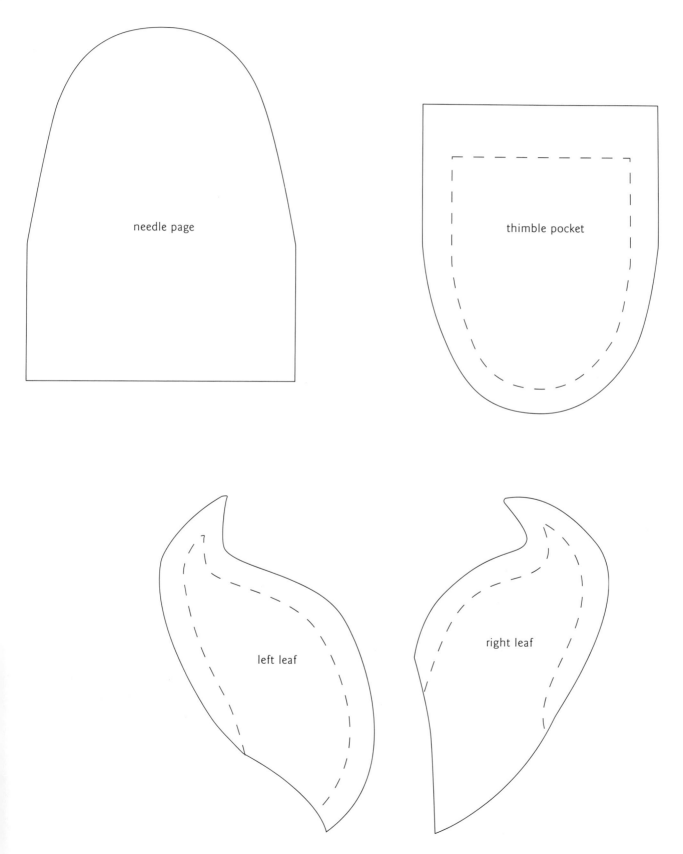

needle page

thimble pocket

left leaf

right leaf

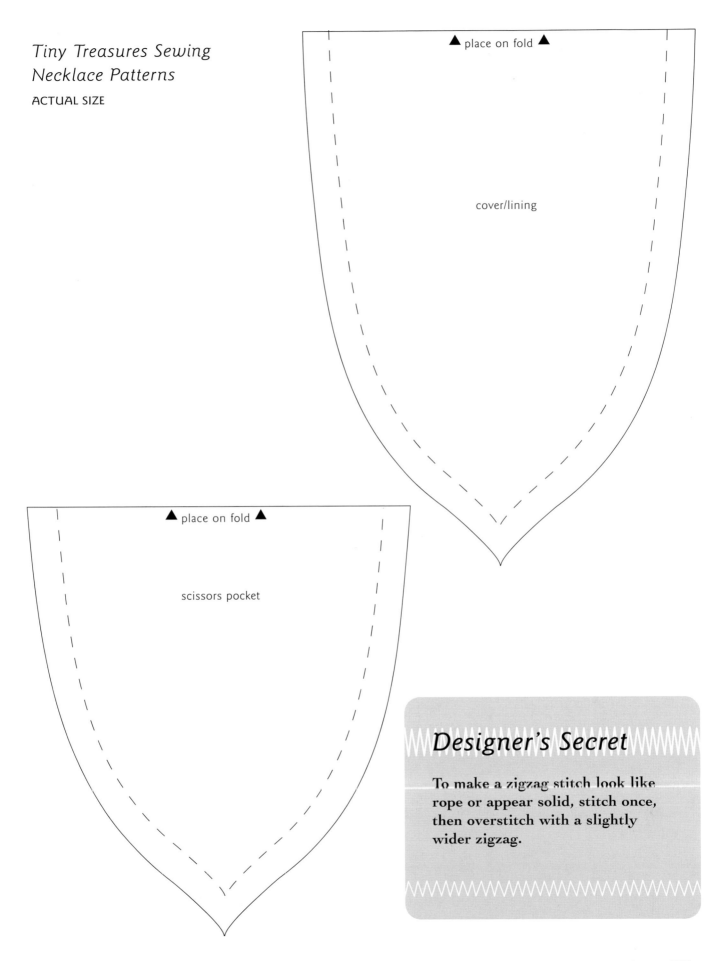

Tiny Treasures Sewing Necklace Patterns

ACTUAL SIZE

▲ place on fold ▲

cover/lining

▲ place on fold ▲

scissors pocket

Designer's Secret

To make a zigzag stitch look like rope or appear solid, stitch once, then overstitch with a slightly wider zigzag.

Scalloped Shell Handbag

Three delicate hues of coral fabric form the shell, and a complementary fabric graces the interior of this pearl-trimmed novelty bag. A novel construction approach lets you complete the appliqué work first, and then the appliqué becomes the bag. Straight and blanket stitching in a variety of colors highlight the curves and offer a dimensional look.

Refer to *Fabrics* and to *Threads* (page 5); to *Stitching* (page 7); to *Stitching Shapes* (page 9); to *Fusible Interfacing* (page 11); and to *Beading* (page 13) before beginning. Test thread colors, stitch lengths, and stitch widths on fabric scraps. Also, check machine tension and practice stitching smoothly around curves with the blanket stitch.

When using any fusible product, always follow the manufacturer's instructions.

Materials

- Lining fabric, ½ yd. (0.5 m)
- Medium-weight fusible interfacing, 1 yd. (0.9 m)
- Fabric A, cotton or special occasion, fat quarter
- Fabric B, cotton or special occasion, fat quarter
- Fabric C, cotton or special occasion, fat quarter
- Threads

- Two strands of pearls, 16" (40.6 cm) long, 4 mm
- Beading thread
- Beading needle
- Button, ½" (1.3 cm)

1 Enlarge all patterns (pages 110 and 111) by 200 percent. Trace the lining/interfacing pattern twice, and bag patterns A, B, and C, including all placement lines, once each.

2 Fold the lining fabric, pin both lining/interfacing patterns against the fold, and cut. Reserve the patterns.

3 Pin patterns A, B, and C to the folded interfacing, matching the fold line to the fold, and cut. Pin the lining/interfacing patterns on the fold, cut the interfacing, and set aside.

4 Adhere interfacings A, B, and C to the wrong side of fabrics A, B, and C. Cut the patterns out, adding a ¼" (6 mm) seam allowance to each pattern.

5 Turn the scalloped edges of fabrics B and C under ¼" (6 mm).

6 Overlap one piece each of A, B, and C, wrong side up, according to the placement diagram. Lay the interfacing on top, sticky side down. Adjust the fabrics until all the pieces align perfectly with the interfacing. Fuse the interfacing to the back of all the pieces at once. Repeat this procedure to create the other side of the bag.

7 Machine blanket stitch around the scallops of pieces B and C, keeping the uprights of the blanket stitch perpendicular to the edges of the curves, and the straight part of the stitch in the ditch. Stitch both sides of the bag lengthwise from the handle to the bottom edge.

8 Pin one piece of lining to one of the bag pieces, right sides together, along the top (handle) edge only. Stitch using a ¼" (6 mm) seam. Clip the curved edges, turn, and press. Repeat with the other side of the bag and lining.

Continued ⸬

Step 6

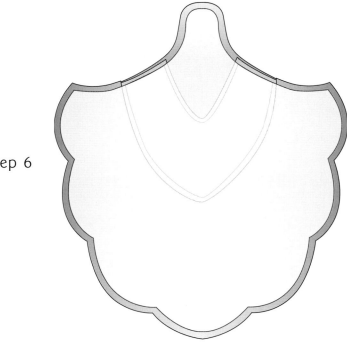

Step 8

Designer's Secret

Lighter colors come forward and darker colors recede. Use darker thread colors in shadows and low areas and lighter colors in front or high areas to give a perceived dimension to the piece.

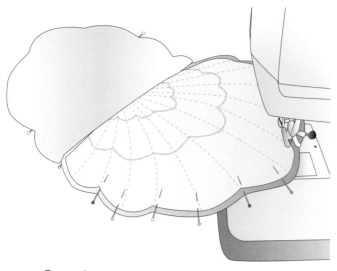

Step 9

9 Pin the bag pieces and the linings, right sides together. Carefully match the seams and pin the seam allowances toward the linings. Stitch, leaving a space for turning. Clip the inner points, and turn the bag.

10 Handstitch the beads along the outer edge seamline. Bring the threaded needle up through the inside, add a bead, go back a bead width and insert the needle, bring up the threaded needle a bead width ahead of the previous bead, and continue. After the beads are added, stitch the opening closed by hand.

11 Work a machine buttonhole on the top of one bag side. Handstitch the button to the top of the other side. If you prefer a buttonless bag, overlap the handle edges and stitch.

Scalloped Shell Handbag Patterns
ENLARGE 200%

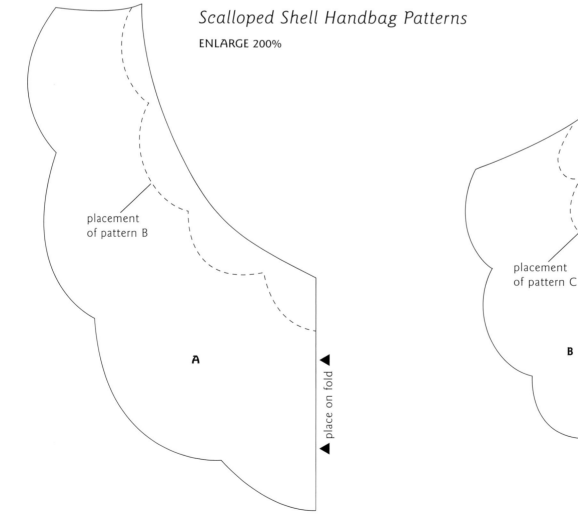

placement of pattern B

A

◄ place on fold ◄

placement of pattern C

B

◄ place on fold ◄

Scalloped Shell Handbag Patterns

SHOWN AT 50%

ENLARGE 200%

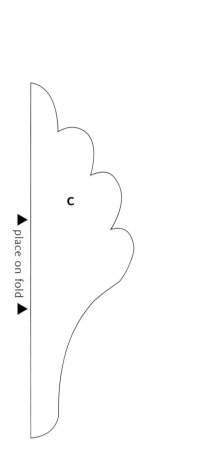

C

▶ place on fold ▶

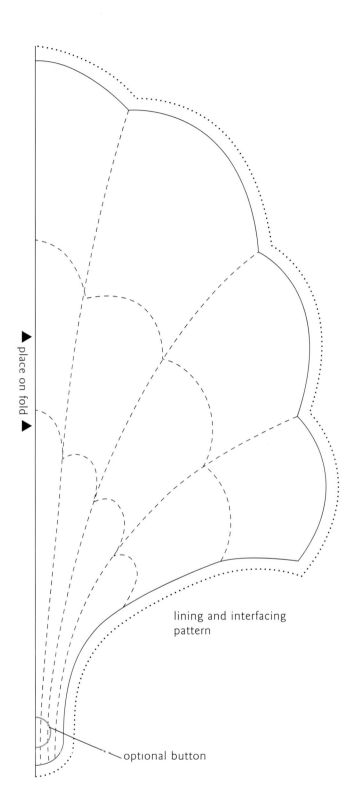

▶ place on fold ▶

lining and interfacing
pattern

optional button

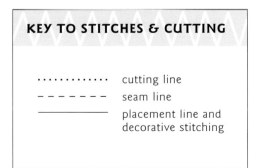

KEY TO STITCHES & CUTTING

· · · · · · · · · · cutting line

– – – – – – seam line

———————— placement line and
decorative stitching

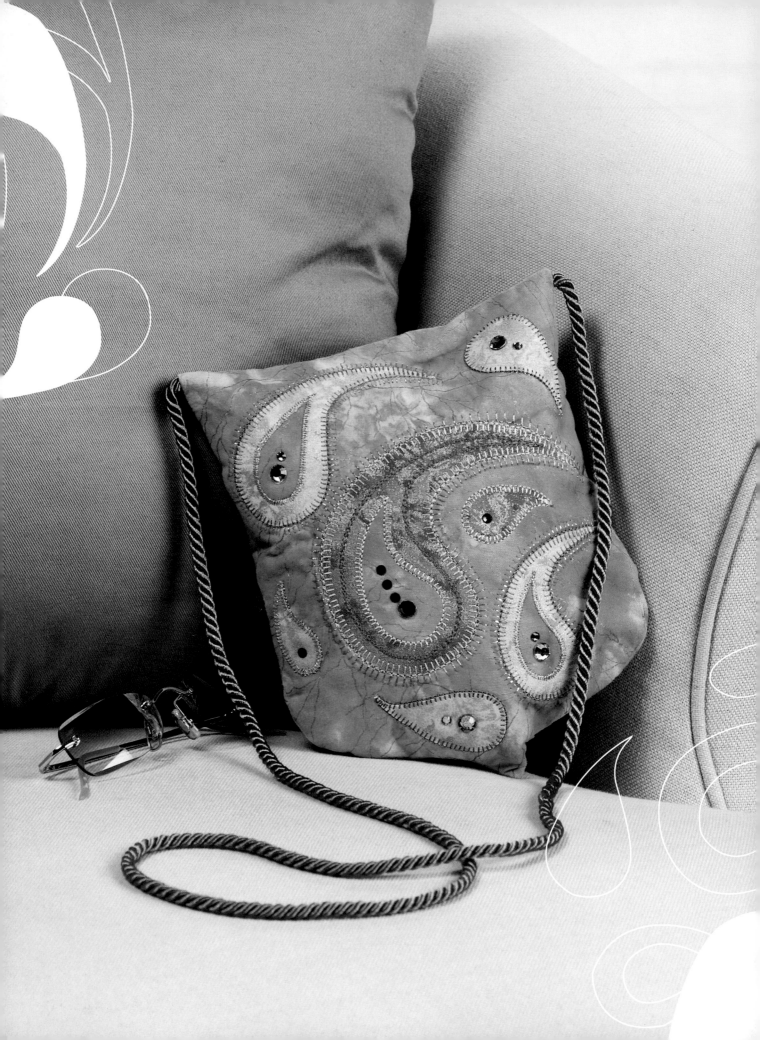

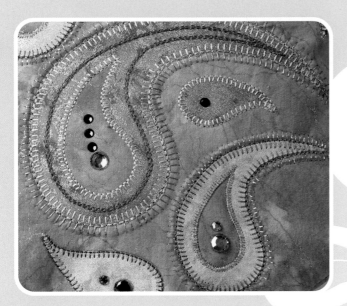

Sassy Shoulder Bag

This eye-catching accessory holds all the essentials. The simple design invites creative choices in thread and embell-ishments, and the clever pockets at back hold your cell phone and sunglasses right at hand.

Refer to *Fabric* and to *Threads* (page 5); to *Crystals* (page 6); to *Stitching* (page 7); to *Stitching Shapes* (page 9); and to *Fusible Web* (page 12) before beginning. Test thread colors, stitch lengths, and stitch widths on fabric scraps.

When using any fusible product, always follow the manufacturer's instructions.

Materials

- Paper-backed fusible web, 8" × 10" (20.3 × 25.4 cm)
- Fabric, gold, 6" (15.2 cm) square
- Fabric, yellow, 8" (20.3 cm) square
- Outer bag and lining fabric, blue, ½ yd. (0.5 m)
- Medium-weight fusible interfacing, 12" × 18" (30.5 × 45.7 cm)
- Threads
- Fourteen crystals, assorted colors, five 7 mm, nine 4 mm
- Zipper, 9" (22.9 cm)
- Cord, blue, 2 yd. (1.8 m)

1 Enlarge all patterns (pages 116 and 117) 125 percent. Trace the cutlines of the gold and yellow shape patterns onto tracing paper and cut them out. Reverse the patterns, place them on the fusible web paper-backing, draw around them, and cut them out. Adhere the web to the wrong side of the appropriate fabrics, leaving the backing intact. Cut the patterns out along the traced lines.

2 Trace the bag and pocket patterns onto tracing paper and cut them out. Using the patterns, cut two of both bag patterns from the blue fabric (lining and outside pieces). Fold the blue fabric, pin the pocket pattern fold line along the fold, and cut one pocket. Cut one of both bag patterns from the fusible interfacing. Fuse the interfacing to the wrong sides of one bag front and one bag back.

3 Place the appliqué shapes on the bag front as they appear in the illustration and fuse in place.

4 Stitch the outside of all shapes with a buttonhole stitch, with the uprights pointing inward. Vary the threads from shape to shape. Stitch around the three largest shapes again, uprights to the outside, using another color of thread. Stitch the inner cutouts of the three large shapes with zigzag stitches. Stitch the center of the largest shape, as shown in the photo, with a forward-and-back machine stitch using a contrasting color thread. Stitch along both sides of the forward-and-back stitching with a straight stitch in a deeper color to create a shadowed effect.

5 Add crystals following the manufacturer's instructions.

6 Place the folded pocket on the back of the bag and stitch down the center line. Fold under the zipper seam on all front and back bag and lining pieces and press. Place the bag front on the zipper and pin. Topstitch the zipper in place. The zipper will hang off the ends, which is fine, as long as the front and back line up properly. Repeat the procedure on the bag back.

7 Cut the shoulder strap cord to the desired length, and baste in place. Open the zipper halfway. Pin the bag front and back, right sides together. Pin the open end of the zipper to the bag back, as if it were closed. Stitch the back and front together, and reinforce the stitching over the cord.

8 Pin the lining back and front, right sides together, leaving a gap for the zipper. Stitch together. Pull the lining over the bag, wrong sides together. Handstitch the lining zipper opening to the zipper. Turn the bag and press lightly.

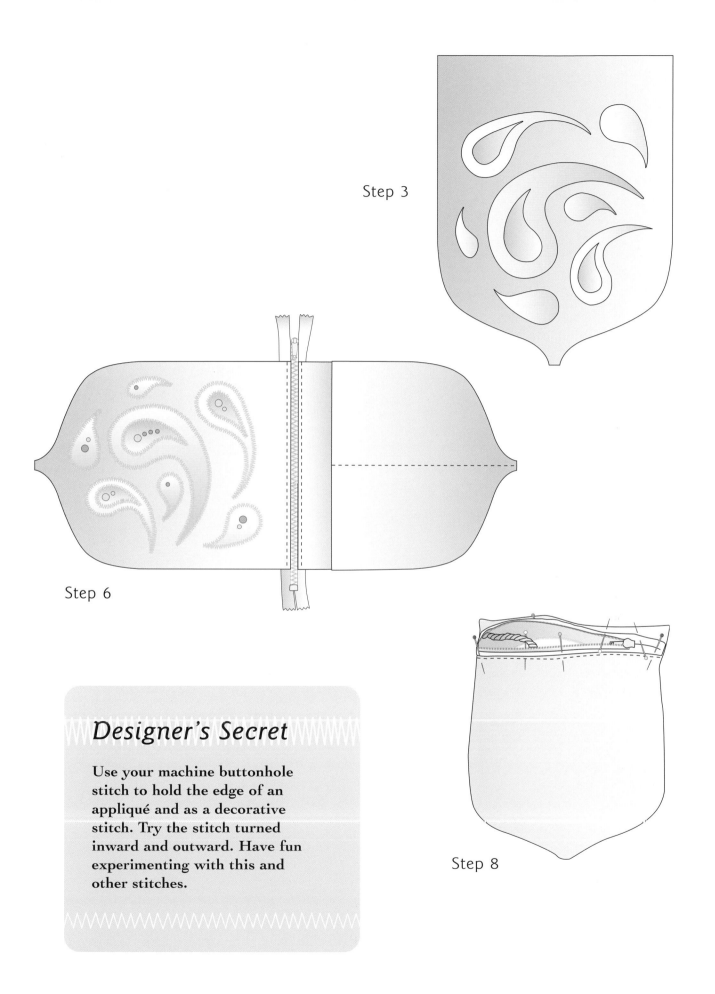

Step 3

Step 6

Designer's Secret

Use your machine buttonhole stitch to hold the edge of an appliqué and as a decorative stitch. Try the stitch turned inward and outward. Have fun experimenting with this and other stitches.

Step 8

Sassy Shoulder Bag Pattern
ENLARGE 125%

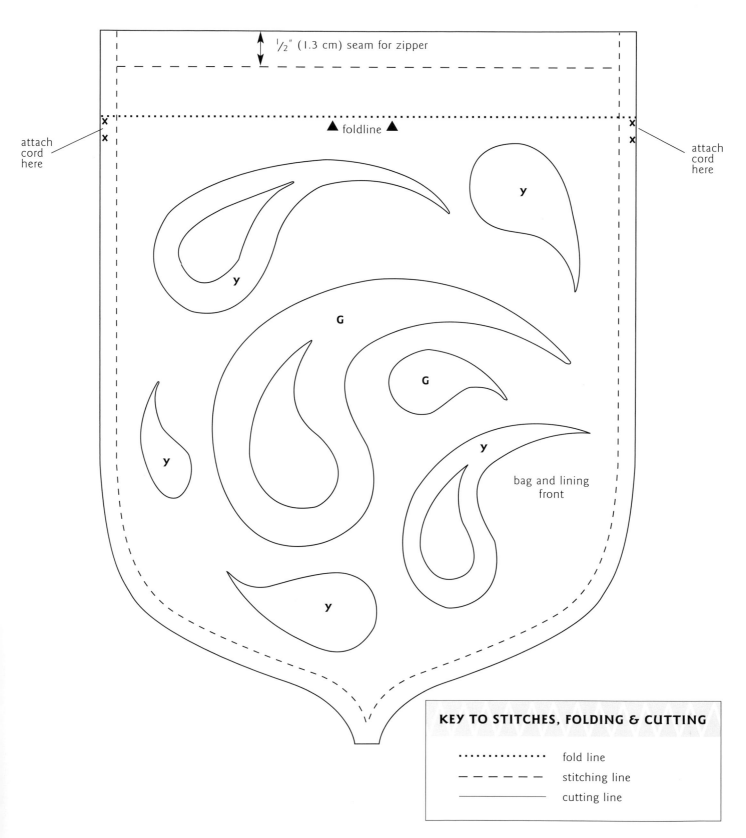

½" (1.3 cm) seam for zipper

▲ foldline ▲

attach cord here

attach cord here

y

y

G

G

y

y

y

bag and lining front

KEY TO STITCHES, FOLDING & CUTTING

············· fold line

− − − − − stitching line

―――― cutting line

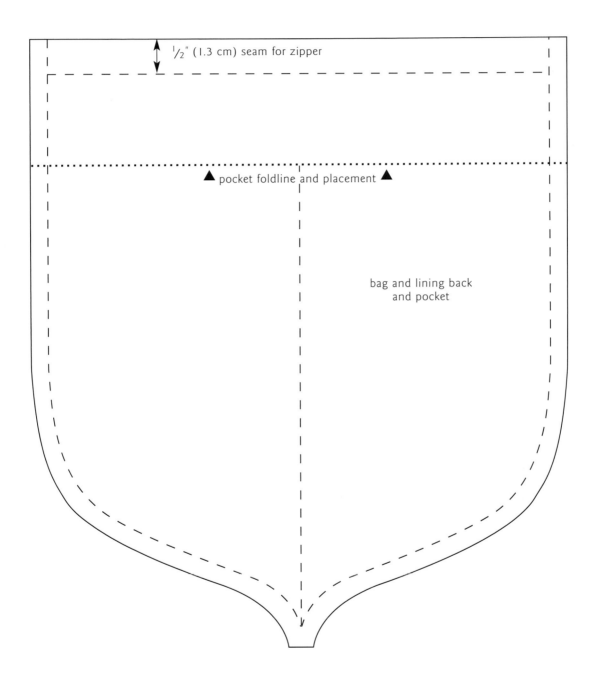

½" (1.3 cm) seam for zipper

▲ pocket foldline and placement ▲

bag and lining back
and pocket

Dragonfly Tee

Add sparkle and whimsy to a purchased sweater to make it uniquely your own. This quick project can be completed in an evening and will show off your talents every time it's worn.

Refer to *Fabrics* and to *Threads* (page 5); *Aerosol Spray Baste, Removable Stabilizers,* and to *Crystals* (page 6); *Pattern Placement Using Tracing Paper* and to *Stitching* (page 7); *Stitching Shapes* (page 9); and to *Fusible Web* (page 12) before beginning. Test thread colors, stitch lengths, and stitch widths on fabric scraps.

When using any fusible product, always follow the manufacturer's instructions.

Materials

- Paper-backed light-weight fusible web, 4" (10.2 cm) square
- Wings fabric, special occasion, 4" (10.2 cm) square
- Aerosol spray baste
- Removable stabilizer, 6" (15.2 cm) square
- Threads
- Crystals, one 7 mm, two 6 mm, four 4 mm

1 Trace the outline of the wing patterns (page 121) onto tracing paper and cut them out. Draw around the patterns on the fusible web paper-backing. Adhere the web to the wrong side of the wings fabric, leaving the backing intact. Cut the pattern out along the traced lines.

2 Trace the entire dragonfly motif (page 121), with the flight path, onto tracing or white tissue paper.

3 Position, then pin, the tracing paper pattern onto the right side of the garment in the desired location. Spritz spray baste on one side of the removable stabilizer. Adhere the stabilizer to the wrong side of the garment in the pattern area, creating a sandwich of tracing paper, garment, and stabilizer. Be sure the stabilizer is under all the stitching areas.

4 Straight stitch the flight path, through the paper, starting under the dragonfly's body. At the end, turn and stitch over first stitching. Pull all the threads to the back, knot, and trim.

5 Position the fabric wings under the tracing paper, using the pattern as a guide. Fuse the wings to the garment. Remove the tracing paper.

6 Zigzag stitch the wings, using a very narrow width on the lower wings and a slightly wider width on the upper wings. Pull all threads to the back, knot, and trim.

7 Adhere the crystals following the manufacturer's instructions. Remove the stabilizer.

Step 1

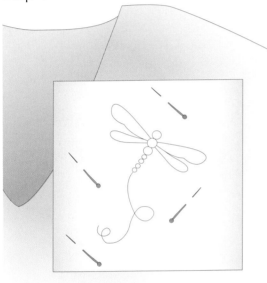

Step 3

Dragonfly Tee Patterns

ACTUAL SIZE

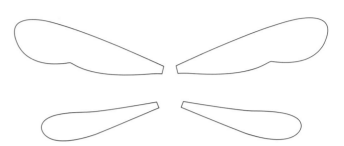

Designer's Secret

To stitch a complex line design onto fabric without marking the fabric, trace the design onto tracing or white tissue paper. Place the paper tracing on the right side of the fabric and pin or spray baste in place. Stitch through the paper, then remove it.

Ring Handle Bag

The flowerlike appliqués, created by layering design elements, give this bag a whimsical flair. Fabric-covered wire ring handles and a bold lining offer stylish sass.

Refer to *Fabrics* and to *Threads* (page 5); to *Light Box* (page 6); to *Stitching* (page 7); to *Stitching Shapes* (page 9); to *Fusible Interfacing* (page 11); and to "Templates," *Freezer Paper* (page 12); before beginning. Test thread colors, stitch lengths, and stitch widths on fabric scraps. Also, check machine tension and practice stitching smoothly around curves with the blanket stitch.

When using any fusible product, always follow the manufacturer's instructions.

Materials

- Light box
- Freezer paper
- Handle and flower petal A fabric, ½ yd. (0.5 m)
- Flower petal B fabric, fat quarter
- Flower petal C fabric, fat quarter
- Spray starch
- Threads

- Medium-weight stiff fusible interfacing, ¾ yd. (0.7 m)
- Bag fabric, 18" × 22" (45.7 × 55.9 cm)
- Gusset and tab fabric, ¼ yd. (0.2 m)
- Lining fabric, ½ yd. (0.5 m)
- Two wire craft rings, 7" (17.8 cm) dia.
- Glue

1 Enlarge the gusset, the bag, and all the flower patterns (pages 126 and 127) 200 percent. Using a light box, trace flower patterns A-1, B-1, and C-1 once and A-2, A-3, B-2, B-3, and C-2 twice onto the dull side of freezer paper, then *label every template*. Fold the freezer paper and cut out the templates creating double the number of templates. Adhere each template to the wrong side of the appropriate fabric, using a warm dry iron. Cut around all the petal templates, adding a ¼" (6 mm) seam allowance. Press under the seam allowances, using a light spray starch and clipping the curves.

2 Remove the freezer paper from all the templates. Lay out all A petals right side up. Place the B petals on top of the A petals, right side up, using the illustration as a guide. Straight stitch close to the edge of the B petals. Place the C petals on top of the B petals, right side up, and stitch around them using a blanket stitch. To reduce bulkiness, you may choose to trim petal A-1 out from under petal B-1.

3 Trace the bag and the gusset patterns twice onto tracing paper. Tape the gusset patterns together at the fold line. Pin the three patterns on the interfacing and cut along the drawn lines. Mark the center line on all the patterns. Fuse the interfacing to the wrong side of the appropriate fabrics, following the manufacturer's instructions. Cut the fabrics, using the interfacing as the pattern, adding a ½" (1.3 cm) seam allowance to all edges. Mark teh center lines.

4 Position the petals on the bag pieces, pin, and then straight stitch close to the edge of petal A. Stitch the top edges of the bag, right sides together, with a ½" (1.3 cm) seam.

5 Cut a 3" × 22" (7.6 × 55.9 cm) strip from the gusset fabric. Fold the right sides together lengthwise and stitch with a ¼" (6 mm) seam. Turn and press with the seam at the center back. Cut eight 2½" (6.4 cm) lengths. Place the front side of a tab on the right side of the bag, using the pattern illustration as a placement guide, and machine baste the end. Repeat for all tabs.

Continued ⫶

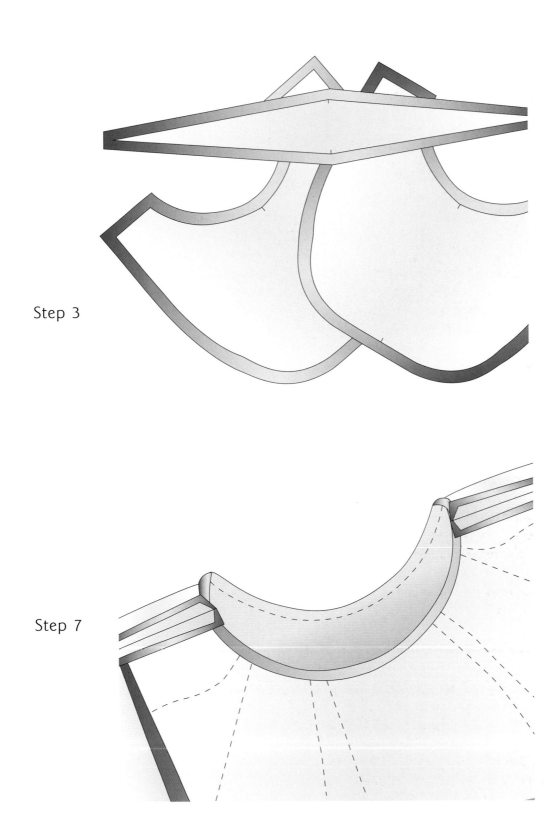

Step 3

Step 7

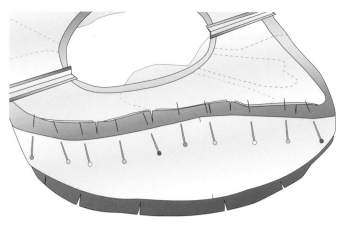

Step 8

Ring Handle Bag Pattern

ENLARGE 200%

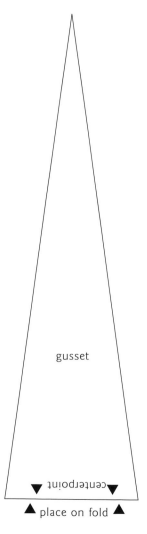

gusset

▲ centerpoint ▲

▲ place on fold ▲

6 Stitch the top edges of the bag, right sides together.

7 Pin the lining to the bag along the front handle edge, right sides together. Stitch along the edge of the interfacing, trim the seams, and clip the curves.

8 Using the center line as a guide, pin the gusset to the bag front, right sides together. Clip the gusset within the seam allowance as needed. Stitch the gusset to the bag along the edge of the interfacing. Repeat this step to attach the gusset to the bag back. Stitch the remaining side seams.

9 Pin the lining to the bag along the back handle edge, right sides together. Stitch along the edge of the interfacing, leaving a place for turning. Trim the seams and clip the curves. Turn the bag. Press the handle edge, if needed. Handstitch the opening closed.

Continued ⫶▸

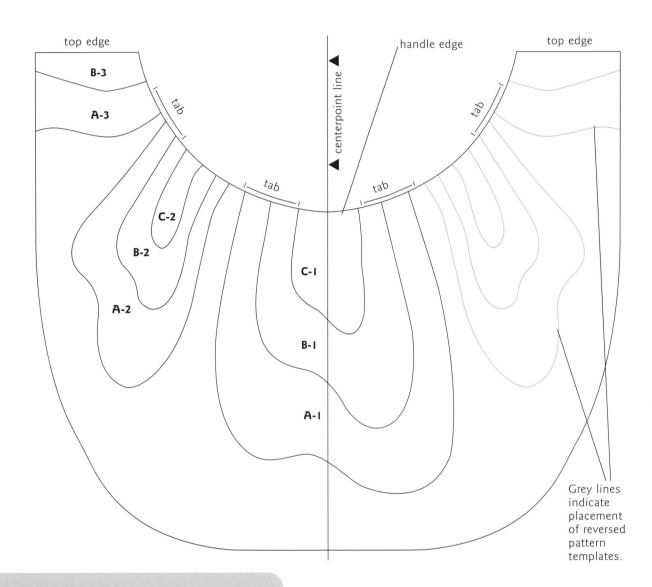

top edge

B-3

A-3

tab

handle edge

▶ centerpoint line ◀

top edge

tab

tab

C-2

B-2

A-2

tab

C-1

B-1

A-1

Grey lines indicate placement of reversed pattern templates.

Designer's Secret

Cut a template and its reverse pattern at the same time! Use a light box to trace the patterns on the dull side of freezer paper. Fold the freezer paper, shiny sides together, and cut.

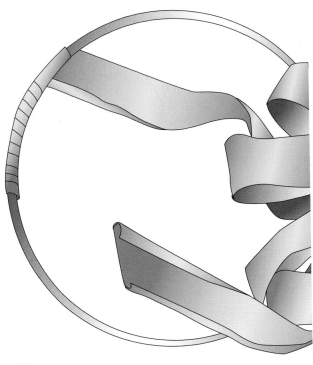

Step 10

10 Press the handle fabric. Square the fabric by trimming all four edges to create right-angled corners. Fold the fabric so the trimmed selvage edge aligns with the crosswise cut. Measure out ¾" (1.9 cm) from the bias fold and cut the first strip. Cut seven more strips 1¼" (3.2 cm) wide. Pin four strips, right sides together, at a right angle and slightly offset. Stitch together using a ¼" (6 mm) seam. Trim the seams to ⅛" (3 mm) and press open. Trim the points of the seams even with the edges. Fold under one long edge ¼" (6 mm) and press. Repeat with the other four strips. The folded edge of the fabric strip creates the finished edge on the handle. Hold one end of the fabric strip on the ring and wind the strip around it, right side to the outside. Overlap each round up to the folded edge. Glue every third wind with a drop of glue near the raw edge. To complete, fold under 3" (7.6 cm) of the remaining long edge ¼" (6 mm) (both long edges of the strip are now folded under) and wind three or four more times. Cut the fabric strip, fold under the cut edge ¼" (6 mm), and handstitch with a blind stitch to secure.

11 Fold the raw edges of the tabs under ¼" (6 mm). Pin, then baste. Place a handle on the front tabs and fold the tabs over to the inside. Handstitch the tabs in place. Repeat to attach the back handle.